Improving Evaluation of Anticrime Programs

Committee on Improving Evaluation of Anti-Crime Programs

Committee on Law and Justice

Division of Behavioral and Social Sciences and Education

NATIONAL RESEARCH COUNCIL
OF THE NATIONAL ACADEMIES

THE NATIONAL ACADEMIES PRESS
Washington, D.C.
www.nap.edu

THE NATIONAL ACADEMIES PRESS 500 Fifth Street, N.W. Washington, DC 20001

NOTICE: The project that is the subject of this report was approved by the Governing Board of the National Research Council, whose members are drawn from the councils of the National Academy of Sciences, the National Academy of Engineering, and the Institute of Medicine. The members of the committee responsible for the report were chosen for their special competences and with regard for appropriate balance.

This study was supported by Contract/Grant No. LJXX-I-03-02-A, between the National Academy of Sciences and the United States Department of Justice. Support of the work of the Committee on Law and Justice is provided by the National Institute of Justice. Any opinions, findings, conclusions, or recommendations expressed in this publication are those of the author(s) and do not necessarily reflect the views of the organizations or agencies that provided support for the project.

International Standard Book Number 0-309-09706-1

Additional copies of this report are available from the National Academies Press, 500 Fifth Street, N.W., Lockbox 285, Washington, DC 20055; (800) 624-6242 or (202) 334-3313 (in the Washington metropolitan area); Internet, http://www.nap.edu

Printed in the United States of America.

Suggested citation: National Research Council. (2005). *Improving Evaluation of Anticrime Programs*. Committee on Improving Evaluation of Anti-Crime Programs. Committee on Law and Justice, Division of Behavioral and Social Sciences and Education. Washington, DC: The National Academies Press.

THE NATIONAL ACADEMIES
Advisers to the Nation on Science, Engineering, and Medicine

The **National Academy of Sciences** is a private, nonprofit, self-perpetuating society of distinguished scholars engaged in scientific and engineering research, dedicated to the furtherance of science and technology and to their use for the general welfare. Upon the authority of the charter granted to it by the Congress in 1863, the Academy has a mandate that requires it to advise the federal government on scientific and technical matters. Dr. Ralph J. Cicerone is president of the National Academy of Sciences.

The **National Academy of Engineering** was established in 1964, under the charter of the National Academy of Sciences, as a parallel organization of outstanding engineers. It is autonomous in its administration and in the selection of its members, sharing with the National Academy of Sciences the responsibility for advising the federal government. The National Academy of Engineering also sponsors engineering programs aimed at meeting national needs, encourages education and research, and recognizes the superior achievements of engineers. Dr. Wm. A. Wulf is president of the National Academy of Engineering.

The **Institute of Medicine** was established in 1970 by the National Academy of Sciences to secure the services of eminent members of appropriate professions in the examination of policy matters pertaining to the health of the public. The Institute acts under the responsibility given to the National Academy of Sciences by its congressional charter to be an adviser to the federal government and, upon its own initiative, to identify issues of medical care, research, and education. Dr. Harvey V. Fineberg is president of the Institute of Medicine.

The **National Research Council** was organized by the National Academy of Sciences in 1916 to associate the broad community of science and technology with the Academy's purposes of furthering knowledge and advising the federal government. Functioning in accordance with general policies determined by the Academy, the Council has become the principal operating agency of both the National Academy of Sciences and the National Academy of Engineering in providing services to the government, the public, and the scientific and engineering communities. The Council is administered jointly by both Academies and the Institute of Medicine. Dr. Ralph J. Cicerone and Dr. Wm. A. Wulf are chair and vice chair, respectively, of the National Research Council.

www.national-academies.org

Preface

B illions of dollars have been spent on crime prevention and control programs over the past decade. However scientifically strong impact evaluations of these programs, while improving, are still uncommon in the context of the overall number of programs that have received funding. The report of the Committee on Improving Evaluation of Anti-Crime Programs is designed as a guide for agencies and organizations responsible for program evaluation, for researchers who must design scientifically credible evaluations of government and privately sponsored programs, and for policy officials who are investing more and more in the concept of evidence-based policy to guide their decisions in crucial areas of crime prevention and control.

The committee could not have completed its work without the help of numerous individuals who participated in the workshop that led to this report. We are especially grateful to the presenters: John Baron, The Council for Excellence in Government; Richard Berk, University of California, Los Angeles; Anthony Braga, Harvard University; Patricia Chamberlain, Oregon Social Learning Center; Adele Harrell, the Urban Institute; Steven Levitt, University of Chicago; Robert Moffitt, Johns Hopkins University; Lawrence Sherman, University of Pennsylvania; Petra Todd, University of Pennsylvania; Alex Wagenaar, University of Minnesota; and Edward Zigler, Yale University. The committee thanks Sarah Hart, the director of the National Institute of Justice, for her ongoing encouragement and interest in our work, Patrick Clark, our program officer, and Betty Chemers, the director of the Evaluation Division, who both provided invaluable guidance as we developed the workshop themes. The committee also thanks all of those who gave of their time and intellectual talents to enrich this report through their participation in the workshop discussion of the papers. We have included biographical sketches of committee members and staff as Appendix A and also a complete list of workshop participants as Appendix B of this report.

This report has been reviewed in draft form by individuals chosen for their diverse perspectives and technical expertise, in accordance with procedures approved by the National Research Council's Report Review Committee. The purpose of this independent review is to provide candid and critical comments that will assist the institution in making its published report as sound as possible and to ensure that the report meets institutional standards for objectivity, evidence, and responsiveness to the study charge. The review comments and draft manuscript remain confidential to protect the integrity of the deliberative process. We wish to thank the following individuals for their review of this report: Philip J. Cook, Department of Public Policy, Duke University; Brian R. Flay, Institute for Health Research and Policy, University of Illinois at Chicago; Rebecca A. Maynard, Graduate School of Education, University of Pennsylvania; Therese D. Pigott, Research Methodology, School of Education, Loyola University, Chicago; Patrick H. Tolan, Institute for Juvenile Research and Department of Psychiatry, University of Illinois at Chicago; and Jack L. Vevea, Department of Psychology, University of California, Santa Cruz.

Although the reviewers listed above have provided many constructive comments and suggestions, they were not asked to endorse the conclusions or recommendations nor did they see the final draft of the report before its release. The review of this report was overseen by Brian Junker, Department of Statistics, Carnegie Mellon University. Appointed by the National Research Council, he was responsible for making certain that an independent examination of this report was carried out in accordance with institutional procedures and that all review comments were carefully considered. Responsibility for the final content of this report rests entirely with the authoring committee and the institution.

Mark W. Lipsey, *Chair*
Committee on Improving
Evaluation of Anti-Crime Programs

Contents

Executive Summary   1

1   Introduction   7

2   What Questions Should the Evaluation Address?   14

3   When Is an Impact Evaluation Appropriate?   22

4   How Should an Impact Evaluation Be Designed?   34

5   How Should the Evaluation Be Implemented?   45

6   What Organizational Infrastructure and Procedures Support
    High-Quality Evaluation?   54

7   Summary, Conclusions, and Recommendations:
    Priorities and Focus   61

References   68

Appendixes

A   Biographical Sketches of Committee Members and Staff   73

B   Participant List: Workshop on Improving Evaluation of
    Criminal Justice Programs   76

Executive Summary

Effective guidance of criminal justice policy and practice requires evidence about their effects on the populations and conditions they are intended to influence. The role of evaluation research is to provide that evidence and to do so in a manner that is accessible and informative to policy makers. Recent criticisms of evaluation research in criminal justice indicate a need for greater attention to the quality of evaluation design and the implementation of evaluation plans.

In the context of concerns about evaluation methods and quality, the National Institute of Justice asked the Committee on Law and Justice of the National Research Council to conduct a workshop on improving the evaluation of criminal justice programs and to follow up with a report that extracts guidance for effective evaluation practices from those proceedings.

The workshop participants presented and discussed examples of evaluation-related studies that represent the methods and challenges associated with research at three levels: interventions directed toward individuals; interventions in neighborhoods, schools, prisons, or communities; and interventions at a broad policy level.

This report highlights major considerations in developing and implementing evaluation plans for criminal justice programs. It is organized around a series of questions that require thoughtful analysis in the development of any evaluation plan.

WHAT QUESTIONS SHOULD THE EVALUATION ADDRESS?

Program evaluation is often taken to mean impact evaluation—assessing the effects of the program on its intended outcomes. However, the concepts and methods of evaluation research include evaluation of other aspects of a program such as the need for the program, its design, implementation, and cost-effectiveness. Questions about program effects are not necessarily the evaluation questions most appropriate to address for all programs, although they are usually the ones with the greatest generality and potential practical significance.

Moreover, evaluations of criminal justice programs may have no practical, policy, or theoretical significance if the program is not sufficiently well developed for the results to have generality or if there is no audience likely to be interested in the results. Allocating limited evaluation resources productively requires careful assignment of priorities to the programs to be evaluated and the questions to be asked about their performance.

• Agencies that sponsor and fund evaluations of criminal justice programs should assess and assign priorities to the evaluation opportunities within their scope. Resources should be directed mainly toward evaluations with the greatest potential for practical and policy significance from expected evaluation results and for which the program circumstances are amenable to productive research.

• For such public agencies as the National Institute of Justice, that process should involve input from practitioners, policy makers, and researchers about the practical significance of the knowledge likely to be generated and the appropriate priorities to apply.

WHEN IS IT APPROPRIATE TO CONDUCT AN IMPACT EVALUATION?

A sponsoring agency cannot launch an impact evaluation with reasonable prospects for success unless the specific program to be evaluated has been identified; background information has been gathered that indicates that evaluation is feasible; and considerations that describe the key issues for shaping the design of the evaluation are identified.

• The requisite background work may be done by an evaluator proposing an evaluation prior to submitting the proposal. To stimulate and capitalize on such situations, sponsoring agencies should consider devoting some portion of the funding available for evaluation to support (a) researchers proposing early stages of evaluation that address issues of priority, feasibility, and evaluability and (b) opportunistic funding of impact evaluations proposed by researchers who find themselves in those fortuitous circumstances that allow a strong evaluation to be conducted of a significant criminal justice program.

• Alternatively, the requisite background work may be instigated by the sponsoring agency for programs judged to be of high priority for impact evaluation. To accomplish this, agencies should undertake feasibility or design studies that will assess whether an impact evaluation is likely to be successful for a program of interest.

• The preconditions for successful impact evaluation are most easily attained when they are built into a program from the start. Agencies that sponsor program initiatives should consider which new programs may be significant candidates for impact evaluation. The program initiative should then be configured to require or encourage as much as possible the inclusion of the well-defined program structures, record-keeping and data collection, documentation of program activities, and other such components supportive of an eventual impact evaluation.

HOW SHOULD AN IMPACT EVALUATION BE DESIGNED?

Evaluation design involves many practical and technical considerations related to sampling and the generalizability of results, statistical power, measurement, methods for estimating program effects, and information that helps explain effects. There are no simple answers to the question of which designs best fit which evaluation situations and all choices inevitably involve tradeoffs between what is desirable and what is practical and between the relative strengths and weaknesses of different methods. Nonetheless, some general guidelines can be applied when considering the approach to be used for a particular impact evaluation.

• A well-developed and clearly-stated Request for Proposals (RFP) is the first step in guarding against implementation failure. When requesting an impact evaluation for a program of interest, the sponsoring agency should specify as completely as possible the evaluation questions to be answered, the program sites expected to participate, the relevant outcomes, and the preferred methods to be used. Agencies should devote sufficient resources during the RFP-development stage, including support for site visits, evaluability assessments, pilot studies, pipeline analyses, and other such preliminary investigations necessary to ensure the development of strong guidance to the field in RFPs.

• Development of the specifications for an impact evaluation (e.g., an RFP) and the review of proposals for conducting the evaluation should involve expert panels of evaluators with diverse methodological backgrounds and sufficient opportunity for them to explore and discuss the trade-offs and potential associated with different approaches.

• In order to strengthen the quality of application reviews, a two-stage review is recommended: the policy relevance of the programs under consideration for evaluation should be first judged by knowledgeable policy makers, practitioners, and researchers. Proposals that pass this screen should then receive a scientific review from a panel of well-qualified researchers, focusing solely on the scientific merit and likelihood of successful implementation of the proposed research.

• Given the state of criminal justice knowledge, randomized experimental designs should be favored in situations where it is likely that they can be implemented with integrity and will yield useful results. This is particularly the case where the intervention is applied to units for which assignment to different conditions is feasible, e.g., individual persons or clusters of moderate scope such as schools or centers.

• Before an impact evaluation design is implemented, the assumptions on which the validity of its results depends should be made explicit, the data and analyses required to support credible conclusions about program effects should be identified, and the availability or feasibility of obtaining the required data should be demonstrated.

HOW SHOULD THE EVALUATION BE IMPLEMENTED?

High-quality evaluation is most likely to occur when (a) the design is tailored to the respective program circumstances in ways that facilitate adequate implementation, (b) the program being evaluated understands, agrees to, and fulfills its role in the evaluation, and (c) problems that arise during implementation are anticipated as much as possible and dealt with promptly and effectively.

• Plans and commitments for impact evaluation should be built into the design of programs during their developmental phase whenever possible.

A detailed management plan should be developed for implementation of an impact evaluation that specifies the key events and activities and associated timeline for both the evaluation team and the program.

• Knowledgeable staff of the sponsoring agency should monitor the implementation of the evaluation.

• Especially for larger projects, implementation and problem solving may be facilitated by support of the evaluation team through such activities as meetings or cluster conferences of evaluators with similar projects for the purpose of cross-project sharing or consultation with advisory groups of veteran researchers.

WHAT ORGANIZATIONAL INFRASTRUCTURE AND PROCEDURES SUPPORT HIGH-QUALITY EVALUATION?

The research methods for conducting an impact evaluation, the data resources needed to adequately support it, and the integration and synthesis of results for policy makers and researchers are all areas in which the basic tools need further development to advance high-quality evaluation of criminal justice programs. Agencies with a major investment in evaluation, such as the National Institute of Justice, should devote a portion of available funds to methodological development in areas such as the following:

• Research aimed at adapting and improving impact evaluation designs for criminal justice applications; for example, development and validation of effective uses of alternative designs such as regression-discontinuity, selection bias models for nonrandomized comparisons, and techniques for modeling program effects with observational data.

• Development and improvement of new and existing databases in ways that would better support impact evaluation of criminal justice programs. Measurement studies that would expand the repertoire of relevant outcome variables and knowledge about their characteristics and relationships for purposes of impact evaluation (e.g., self-report delinquency and criminality; official records of arrests, convictions, and the like; measures of critical mediators).

• Synthesis and integration of the findings of impact evaluations in ways that would inform practitioners and policy makers about the effectiveness of different types of criminal justice programs and the characteristics of the most effective programs of each type and that would inform researchers about gaps in the research and the influence of methodological variation on evaluation results.

To support high-quality impact evaluation, the sponsoring agency must itself incorporate and maintain sufficient expertise to set effective and feasible evaluation priorities, manage the background preparation necessary to develop the specifications for evaluation projects, monitor implementation, and work well with expert advisory boards and review panels.

• Agencies that sponsor a significant portfolio of evaluation research in criminal justice, such as the National Institute of Justice, should maintain a separate evaluation unit with clear responsibility for developing and completing high-quality evaluation projects. To be effective, such a unit will generally need a dedicated budget, some authority over evaluation research budgets and projects, and independence from undue program and political influence on the nature and implementation of the evaluation projects undertaken.

• The agency personnel responsible for developing and overseeing impact evaluation projects should include individuals with relevant research backgrounds who are assigned to evaluation functions and maintained in those positions in ways that ensure continuity of experience with the challenges of criminal justice evaluation, methodological developments, and the community of researchers available to conduct quality evaluations.

• The unit and personnel responsible for developing and completing evaluation projects should be supported by review and advisory panels that provide expert consultation in developing RFPs, reviewing evaluation proposals and plans, monitoring the implementation of evaluation studies, and other such functions that must be performed well in order to facilitate high-quality evaluation research.

1

Introduction

T his is an especially opportune time to consider current practices and future prospects for the evaluation of criminal justice programs. In recent years there have been increased calls from policy makers for "evidence-based practice" in health and human services that have extended to criminal justice as, for example, in the joint initiative of the Office of Justice Programs and the Coalition for Evidence-Based Policy on evidence-based crime and substance-abuse policy.[1] This trend has been accompanied by various organized attempts to use the findings of evaluation research to determine "what works" in criminal justice. The Maryland Report (Sherman et al., 1997) responded to a request by Congress to review existing research and identify effective programs and practices. The Crime and Justice Group of the Campbell Collaboration has embarked on an ambitious effort to develop systematic reviews of research on the effectiveness of crime and justice programs. The OJJDP Blueprints for Violence Prevention project identifies programs whose effectiveness is demonstrated by evaluation research and other lists of programs alleged to be effective on the basis of research have proliferated (e.g., the National Registry of Effective Programs sponsored by the Substance Abuse and Mental Health Services Administration). In addition, the National Research

---

[1]Available: http://www. excelgov.org/displayContent.asp?Keyword=prppcPrevent.

Council's (NRC) Committee on Law and Justice has been commissioned to prepare reports assessing research evidence on such topics as the effectiveness of policing policies (NRC, 2004), firearms policies (NRC, 2005), illicit drug policies (NRC, 2001), and the prevention, treatment, and control of juvenile crime (NRC and Institute of Medicine, 2001).

These developments reflect recognition that effective guidance of criminal justice policy and practice requires evidence about the effects of those policies and practices on the populations and conditions they are intended to influence. For example, knowledge of the ability of various programs to reduce crime or protect potential victims allows resources to be allocated in ways that support effective programs and efficiently promote these outcomes. The role of evaluation research is to provide evidence about these kinds of program effects and to do so in a manner that is accessible and informative to policy makers. Fulfilling that function, in turn, requires that evaluation research be designed and implemented in a manner that provides valid and useful results of sufficient quality to be relied upon by policy makers.

In this context especially, significant methodological shortcomings would seriously compromise the value of evaluation research. And, it is methodological issues that are at the heart of what has arguably been the most influential stimulus for attention to the current state of evaluation research in criminal justice. A series of reports[2] by the U.S. General Accounting Office has been sharply critical of the evaluation studies conducted under the auspices of the Department of Justice. Because several offices within the Department of Justice are major funders of evaluation research on criminal justice programs, especially the larger and more influential evaluation projects, this is a matter of concern not only to the Department of Justice, but to others who conduct and sponsor criminal justice evaluation research.

CRITICISMS OF METHOD

The GAO reports focus on impact evaluation, that is, assessment of the effects of programs on the populations or conditions they are intended

---

[2]*Juvenile Justice: OJJDP Reporting Requirements for Discretionary and Formula Grantees and Concerns About Evaluation Studies* (GAO, 2001). *Drug Courts: Better DOJ Data Collection and Evaluation Efforts Needed to Measure Impact of Drug Court Programs* (GAO, 2002a). *Justice Impact Evaluations: One Byrne Evaluation Was Rigorous; All Reviewed Violence Against Women Office Evaluations Were Problematic* (GAO, 2002b). *Violence Against Women Office: Problems with Grant Monitoring and Concerns About Evaluation Studies* (GAO, 2002c). *Justice Outcome Evaluations: Design and Implementation of Studies Require More NIJ Attention* (GAO, 2003a). *Program Evaluation: An Evaluation Culture and Collaborative Partnerships Help Build Agency Capacity* (GAO, 2003b).

to change. The impact evaluations selected for review cover a wide range of programs, most of which are directed toward a particular criminal justice problem or population and implemented in multiple sites (see Box 1-1). As such, these programs are relatively representative of the kinds of initiatives that a major funder of criminal justice programs might support and wish to evaluate for impact.

The GAO review of the design and implementation of the impact evaluations for these programs identified a number of problem areas that highlight the major challenges that must be met in a sound impact evaluation. These generally fell into two categories: (a) deficiencies in the evaluation design and procedures that were initially proposed and (b) difficulties implementing the evaluation plan. It is indicative of the magnitude of the challenge posed by impact evaluation at this scale that, of the 30 evaluations for the programs shown in Box 1-1, one or both of these problems were noted for 20 of them, and some of the remaining 10 were still in the proposal stage and had not yet been implemented.

The most frequent deficiencies in the initial plan or the implementation of the evaluation identified in the GAO reviews were as follows:

- The sites selected to participate in the evaluation were not representative of the sites that had received the program.
- The program participants selected at the evaluation sites were not representative of the population the program served.
- Pre-program baseline data on key outcome variables were not included in the design or could not be collected as planned so that change over time could not be assessed.
- The intended program outcomes (e.g., reduced criminal activity, drug use, or victimization in contrast to intermediate outcomes such as increases in knowledge) were not measured or outcome measures with doubtful reliability and validity were used.
- No means for isolating program effects from the influence of external factors on the outcomes, such as a nonparticipant comparison group or appropriate statistical controls, were included in the design or the planned procedure could not be implemented.
- The program and comparison groups differed on outcome-related characteristics at the beginning of the program or became different due to differential attrition before the outcomes were measured.
- Data collection was problematic; needed data could not be obtained or response rates were low when it was likely that those who responded differed from those who did not.

No recent review of evaluation research in the general criminal justice literature provides an assessment of methodology that is as compre-

---

BOX 1-1
Programs Represented in the Impact Evaluation Plans and
Projects Reviewed in Recent GAO Reports

Arrest Policies Program (treating domestic violence as a serious violation of law)

Breaking the Cycle (comprehensive service for adult offenders with drug-use histories)

Chicago's Citywide Community Policing Program (policing organized around small geographic areas)

Children at Risk Program (comprehensive services for high-risk youth)

Comprehensive Gang Initiative (community-based program to reduce gang-related crime)

Comprehensive Service-Based Intervention Strategy in Public Housing (program to reduce drug activity and crime)

Corrections and Law Enforcement Family Support (CLEFS) (stress intervention programs for law enforcement officers and families)

Court Monitoring and Batterer Intervention Programs (batterer counseling programs and court monitoring)

Culturally Focused Batterer Counseling for African-American Men

Domestic Violence Victims' Civil Legal Assistance Program (legal services for victims of domestic violence)

Drug Courts (specialized court procedures and services for drug offenders)

Enforcement of Underage Drinking Laws Program

Gang Resistance Education and Training (GREAT) Program (school-based gang prevention program)

Intensive Aftercare (programs for juvenile offenders after release from confinement)

Juvenile Justice Mental Health Initiative (mental health services to families

---

hensive as that represented in the collection of GAO reports summarized above. What does appear in that literature in recent years is considerable discussion of the role and applicability of randomized field experiments for investigating program effects. In Feder and Boruch (2000), a special issue of *Crime and Delinquency* was devoted to the potential for experiments in criminal justice settings, followed a few years later by a special issue (Weisburd, 2003) of *Evaluation Review* on randomized trials in criminology. More recently, a new journal, *Experimental Criminology*, was launched with an explicit focus on experimental and quasi-experimental research for investigating crime and justice practice and policy. The view that research on the effects of criminal justice interventions would be improved by greater emphasis on randomized experiments, however, is by of delinquent youths with serious emotional disturbances)

Juvenile Mentoring Program (volunteer adult mentors for at-risk youth)

Multi-Site Demonstration for Enhanced Judicial Oversight of Domestic Violence Cases (coordinated response to domestic violence offenses)

Multi-Site Demonstration of Collaborations to Address Domestic Violence and Child Maltreatment (community-based programs for coordinated response to families with co-occurring domestic violence and child maltreatment)

Parents Anonymous (support groups for child abuse prevention)

Partnership to Reduce Juvenile Gun Violence Program (coordinated community strategies for selected areas in cities)

Project PATHE (school-based violence prevention)

Reducing Non-Emergency Calls to 911: Four Approaches

Responding to the Problem Police Officer: Early Warning Systems (identification and treatment for officers whose behavior is problematic)

Rural Domestic Violence and Child Victimization Enforcement Grant Program (coordinated strategies for responding to domestic violence)

Rural Domestic Violence and Child Victimization Grant Program (cooperative community-based efforts to reduce domestic violence, dating violence, and child abuse)

Rural Gang Initiative (community-based gang prevention programs)

Safe Schools/Healthy Students (school services to promote healthy development and prevent violence and drug abuse)

Safe Start Initiative (integrated service delivery to reduce impact of family and community violence on young children)

STOP Grant Programs (culture-specific strategies to reduce violence against Indian women)

Victim Advocacy with a Team Approach (domestic violence teams to assist victims)

no means universal. The limitations of experimental methods for such purposes and alternatives using econometric modeling have also received critical attention (e.g., Heckman and Robb, 1985; Manski, 1996).

OVERVIEW OF THE WORKSHOP AND THIS REPORT

In the context of these various concerns about evaluation methods and quality, the National Institute of Justice asked the NRC Committee on Law and Justice to organize a workshop on improving the evaluation of criminal justice programs and to follow up with a report that extracted guidance for effective evaluation practices from those proceedings. The Academies appointed a small steering committee to guide workshop development. The workshop was held in September 2003, and this report is the result of the efforts of the steering committee to further develop the themes raised there and integrate them as constructive advice about conducting evaluations of criminal justice programs.

The purpose of the Workshop on Improving the Evaluation of Criminal Justice Programs was to foster broader implementation of credible evaluations in the field of criminal justice by promoting informed discussion of:

- the repertoire of applicable evaluation methods;
- issues in matching methods to program and policy circumstances; and
- the organizational infrastructure requirements for supporting sound evaluation.

This purpose was pursued through presentation and discussion of case examples of evaluation-related studies selected to represent the methods and challenges associated with research at each of three different levels of intervention. The three levels are distinguished by different social units that are the target of intervention and thus constitute the units of analysis for the evaluation design. The levels and the exemplary evaluation studies and assigned discussant for each were as follows:

(1) Interventions directed toward individuals, a situation in which there are generally a relatively large number of units within the scope of the program being evaluated and potential for assigning those units to different intervention conditions.

- Multidimensional Family Foster Care (Patricia Chamberlain)
- A Randomized Experiment: Testing Inmate Classification Systems (Richard Berk)
- Discussant (Adele Harrell)

(2) Interventions with neighborhoods, schools, prisons, or communities, a situation generally characterized by relatively few units within the scope of the program and often limited potential for assigning those units to different intervention conditions.

- Hot Spots Policing and Crime Prevention (Anthony Braga)
- Communities Mobilizing for Change (Alex Wagenaar)
- Discussant (Edward Zigler)

INTRODUCTION 13

(3) Interventions at the broad local, state, or national level where the program scope encompasses a macro unit and there is virtually no potential for assigning units to different intervention conditions.

- An Empirical Analysis of LOJACK (Steven Levitt)
- Racial Bias in Motor Vehicle Searches (Petra Todd)
- Discussant (John V. Pepper)

After the research case studies in each category were presented, their implications for conducting high-quality evaluations were discussed. A final panel at the end of the workshop then discussed the infrastructure requirements for strong evaluations.

- Infrastructure Requirements for Consumption (and Production) of Strong Evaluations (Lawrence Sherman)
- Recommendations for Evaluation (Robert Moffitt)
- Bringing Evidence-Based Policy to Substance Abuse and Criminal Justice (Jon Baron)

Papers presented at the workshop are provided on the Committee on Law and Justice Website at http://www7.nationalacademies.org/claj/.

The intent of this report is not to summarize the workshop but, rather, to draw upon its contents to highlight the major considerations in developing and implementing evaluation plans for criminal justice programs. In particular, the report is organized around five interrelated questions that require thoughtful analysis in the development of any evaluation plan, with particular emphasis on impact evaluation:

1. What questions should the evaluation address?
2. When is it appropriate to conduct an impact evaluation?
3. How should an impact evaluation be designed?
4. How should the evaluation be implemented?
5. What organizational infrastructure and procedures support high-quality evaluation?

In the pages that follow, each of these questions is examined and advice is distilled from the workshop presentations and discussion, and from subsequent committee deliberations, for answering them in ways that will help improve the evaluation of criminal justice programs. The intended audience for this report includes NIJ, the workshop sponsor and a major funder of criminal justice evaluations, but also other federal, state, and local agencies, foundations, and other such organizations that plan, sponsor, or administer evaluations of criminal justice programs.

2

What Questions Should the Evaluation Address?

C riminal justice programs arise in many different ways. Some are developed by researchers or practitioners and fielded rather narrowly at first in demonstration projects. The practice of arresting perpetrators of domestic violence when police were called to the scene began in this fashion (Sherman, 1992). Others spring into broad acceptance as a result of grass roots enthusiasm, such as Project DARE with its use of police officers to provide drug prevention education in schools. Still others, such as intensive probation supervision, arise from the challenges of everyday criminal justice practice. Our concern in this report is not with the origins of criminal justice programs but with their evaluation when questions about their effectiveness arise among policy makers, practitioners, funders, or sponsors of evaluation research.

The evaluation of such programs is often taken to mean impact evaluation, that is, an assessment of the effects of the program intervention on the intended outcomes (also called outcome evaluation). This is a critical issue for any criminal justice program and its stakeholders. Producing beneficial effects (and avoiding harmful ones) is the central purpose of most programs and the reason for investing resources in them. For this reason, all the subsequent chapters of this report discuss various aspects of impact evaluation.

It does not follow, however, that every evaluation should automatically focus on impact questions (Rossi, Lipsey, and Freeman, 2004; Weiss, 1998). Though important, those questions may be premature in light of limited knowledge about other aspects of program performance that are prerequisites for producing the intended effects. Or, they may be inappropriate in the context of issues with greater political salience or more relevance to the concerns of key audiences for the evaluation.

In particular, questions about aspects of program performance other than impact that may be important to answer in their own right, or in conjunction with addressing impact questions, include the following:

1. Questions about the need for the program, e.g., the nature and magnitude of the problem the program addresses and the characteristics of the population served. Assessment of the need for a program deals with some of the most basic evaluation questions—whether there is a problem that justifies a program intervention and what characteristics of the problem make it more or less amenable to intervention. For a program to reduce gang-related crime, for instance, it is useful to know how much crime is gang-related, what crimes, in what neighborhoods, and by which gangs.

2. Questions about program conceptualization or design, e.g., whether the program targets the appropriate clientele or social units, embodies an intervention that could plausibly bring about the desired changes in those units and involves a delivery system capable of applying the intervention to the intended units. Assessment of the program design examines the soundness of the logic inherent in the assumption that the intervention as intended can bring about positive change in the social conditions to which it is directed. One might ask, for instance, whether it is a sound assumption that prison visitation programs for juvenile offenders, such as Scared Straight, will have a deterrent effect for impressionable antisocial adolescents (Petrosino et al., 2003a).

3. Questions about program implementation and service delivery, e.g., whether the intended intervention is delivered to the intended clientele in sufficient quantity and quality, if the clients believe they benefit from the services, and how well administrative, organizational, personnel, and fiscal functions are handled. Assessment of program implementation, often called process evaluation, is a core evaluation function aimed at determining how well the program is operating, especially whether it is actually delivering enough of the intervention to have a reasonable chance of producing effects. With a program for counseling victims of domestic violence, for example, an evaluation might consider the number of eligible victims who participate, attendance at the counseling sessions, and the quality of the counseling provided.

4. Questions about program cost and efficiency, e.g., what the program costs are per unit of service, whether the program costs are reasonable in relation to the services provided or the magnitude of the intended benefits, and if alternative approaches would yield equivalent benefits at equal or lower cost. Cost and efficiency questions about the delivery of

services relate to important policy and management functions even without evidence that those services actually produce benefits. Cost-benefit and cost-effectiveness assessments are especially informative, however, when they build on the findings of impact evaluation to examine the cost required to attain whatever effects the program produces. Cost questions for a drug court, for instance, might ask how much it costs per offender served and the cost for each recidivistic drug offense prevented.

The design and implementation of impact evaluations capable of producing credible findings about program effects are challenging and often costly. It may not be productive to undertake them without assurance that there is a well-defined need for the program, a plausible program concept for bringing about change, and sufficient implementation of the program to potentially have measurable effects. Among these, program implementation is especially critical. In criminal justice contexts, the organizational and administrative demands associated with delivering program services of sufficient quality, quantity, and scope to bring about meaningful change are considerable. Offenders often resist or manipulate programs, victims may feel threatened and distrustful, legal and administrative factors constrain program activities, and crime, by its nature, is difficult to control. Under these circumstances, programs are often implemented in such weak form that significant effects cannot be expected.

Information about the nature of the problem a program addresses, the program concept for bringing about change, and program implementation are also important to provide an explanatory context within which to interpret the results of an impact evaluation. Weak effects from a poorly implemented program leave open the possibility that the program concept is sound and better outcomes would occur if implementation were improved. Weak effects from a well-implemented program, however, are more likely to indicate theory failure—the program concept or approach itself may be so flawed that no improvement in implementation would produce the intended effects. Even when positive effects are found, it is generally useful to know what aspects of the program circumstances might have contributed to producing those effects and how they might be strengthened. Absent this information, we have what is often referred to as a "black box" evaluation—we know if the expected effects occurred but have no information about how or why they occurred or guidance for how to improve on them.

An important step in the evaluation process, therefore, is developing the questions the evaluation is to answer and ensuring that they are appropriate to the program circumstances and the audience for the evaluation. The diversity of possible evaluation questions that can be addressed and the importance of determining which should be addressed in any given evaluation have several implications for the design and management of evaluation research. Some of the more important of those implications are discussed below.

EVALUATIONS CAN TAKE MANY DIFFERENT FORMS

Evaluations that focus on different questions, assess different programs in different circumstances, and respond to the concerns of different audiences generally require different designs and methods. There will thus be no single template or set of criteria for how evaluations should be conducted or what constitutes high quality. That said, however, there are several recognizable forms of evaluation to which similar design and quality standards apply (briefly described in Box 2-1).

A common and significant distinction is between evaluations concerned primarily with program process and implementation and those focusing on program effects. Process evaluations address questions about how and how well a program functions in its use of resources and delivery of services. They are typically designed to collect data on selected performance indicators that relate to the most critical of these functions, for instance, the amount, quality, and coverage of services provided. These performance indicators are assessed against administrative goals, contractual obligations, legal requirements, professional norms, and other such applicable standards. The relevant performance dimensions, indicators, and standards will generally be specific to the particular program. Thus this form of evaluation will be tailored to the program being evaluated and will show little commonality across programs that are not replicates of each other.

Process evaluations may assess program performance at one point in time or be configured to produce periodic reports on program performance, generally referred to as "performance monitoring." In the latter case, the procedures for collecting and reporting data on performance indicators are often designed by an evaluation specialist but then routinized in the program as a management information system (MIS). When conducted as a one-time assessment, however, process evaluations are generally the responsibility of a designated evaluation team. In that case, assessment of program implementation may be the main aim of the evaluation, or it may be integrated with an impact evaluation.

Program performance monitoring sometimes involves indicators of program outcomes. This situation must be distinguished from impact evaluation because it does not answer questions about the program's effects on those outcomes. A performance monitoring scheme, for instance, might routinely gather information about the recidivism rates of the of-

---

BOX 2-1
Major Forms of Program Evaluation

Process or Implementation Evaluation

An assessment of how well a program functions in its use of resources, delivery of the intended services, operation and management, and the like. Process evaluation may also examine the need for the program, the program concept, or cost.

Performance Monitoring

A continuous process evaluation that produces periodic reports on the program's performance on a designated set of indicators and is often incorporated into program routines as a form of management information system. It may include monitoring of program outcome indicators but does not address the program impact on those outcomes.

Impact Evaluation

An assessment of the effects produced by the program; that is, the outcomes for the target population or settings brought about by the program that would not have occurred otherwise. Impact evaluation may also incorporate cost-effectiveness analysis.

Evaluability Assessment

An assessment of the likely feasibility and utility of conducting an evaluation made before the evaluation is designed. It is used to inform decisions about whether an evaluation should be undertaken and, if so, what form it should take.

---

fenders treated by the program. This information describes the postprogram status of the offenders with regard to their reoffense rates and may be informative if it shows higher or lower rates than expected for the population being treated or interesting changes over time. It does not, however, reveal the program impact on recidivism, that is, what change in recidivism results from the program intervention and would not have occurred otherwise.

Impact evaluations, in turn, are oriented toward determining whether a program produces the intended outcomes, for instance, reduced recidivism among treated offenders, decreased stress for police officers, less trauma for victims, lower crime rates, and the like. The programs that are evaluated may be demonstration programs, such as the early forms of Multidimensional Treatment Foster Care Program (Chamberlain, 2003), that are not widely implemented and which may be mounted or supervised by researchers to find out if they work (often called *efficacy* studies). Or they may involve programs already rather widely used in practice, such as drug courts, that operate with representative personnel, training, client selection, and the like (often called *effectiveness* studies). Such differences in the program circumstances, and many other program variations, influence the nature of the evaluation, which must always be at least somewhat responsive to those circumstances. For present purposes, we will focus on broader considerations that apply across the range of criminal justice impact evaluations.

EVALUATION MUST OFTEN BE PROGRAMMATIC

Determining the priority evaluation questions for a program or group of programs may itself require some investigation into the program circumstances, stakeholder concerns, utility of the expected information, and the like. Moreover, in some instances it may be necessary to have the answers to some questions before asking others. For instance, with relatively new programs, it may be important to establish that the program has reached an adequate level of implementation before embarking on an outcome evaluation. A community policing program, for instance, could require changes in well-established practices that may occur slowly or not at all. In addition, any set of evaluation results will almost inevitably raise additional significant questions. These may involve concerns, for example, about why the results came out the way they did, what factors were most associated with program effectiveness, what side effects might have been missed, whether the effects would replicate in another setting or with a different population, or whether an efficacious program would prove effective in routine practice.

It follows that producing informative, useful evaluation results may require a series of evaluation studies rather than a single study. Such a sustained effort, in turn, requires a relatively long time period over which the studies will be supported and continuity in their planning, implementation, and interpretation.

EVALUATION MAY NOT BE FEASIBLE OR USEFUL

The nature of a program, the circumstances in which it is situated, or the available resources (including time, data, program cooperation, and evaluation expertise) may be such that evaluation is not feasible for a particular program. Alternatively, the evaluation questions it is feasible to answer for the program may not be useful to any identifiable audience. Unfortunately, evaluation is often commissioned and well under way before these conditions are discovered.

The technique of *evaluability assessment* (Wholey, 1994) was developed as a diagnostic procedure evaluators could use to find out if a program was amenable to evaluation and, if so, what form of evaluation would provide the most useful information to the intended audience. A typical evaluability assessment considers how well defined the program is, the availability of performance data, the resources required, and the needs and interests of the audience for the evaluation. Its purpose is to inform decisions about whether an evaluation should be undertaken and, if so, what form it should take. For an agency wishing to plan and commission an evaluation, especially of a large, complex, or diffuse program, a preliminary evaluability assessment can provide background information useful for defining what questions the evaluation should address, what form it should take, and what resources will be required to successfully complete it. Evaluability assessments are discussed in more detail in Chapter 3.

EVALUATION PLANS MUST BE WELL-SPECIFIED

The diversity of potential evaluation questions and approaches that may be applicable to any program allows much room for variation from one evaluation team to another. Agencies that commission and sponsor evaluations will experience this variation if the specifications for the evaluations they fund are not spelled out precisely. Such mechanisms as Requests for Proposals (RFPs) and scope of work statements in contracts are often the initial forms of communication between evaluation sponsors and evaluators about the questions the evaluation will answer and the form it will take. Sponsors who clearly specify the questions of interest and the form in which they expect the answers are more likely to obtain the information they want from an evaluation. At the same time, an evaluation must be responsive to unanticipated events and circumstances in the field that necessitate changes in the plan. It is advantageous, therefore, for the evaluation plan to be both well-specified and also to have provisions for adaptation and renegotiation when needed.

Development of a well-specified evaluation solicitation and plan shifts much of the burden for identifying the focal evaluation questions and the form of useful answers to the evaluation sponsor. More often, in contrast, the sponsor provides only general guidelines and relies on the applicants to shape the specific questions and approach. For the sponsor to be proactive in defining the evaluation focus, the sponsoring agency and personnel must have the capacity to engage in thoughtful planning prior to commissioning the evaluation. That, in turn, may require some preliminary investigation of the program circumstances, the policy context, feasibility, and the like. When a programmatic approach to evaluation is needed, the planning process must take a correspondingly long-term perspective, with associated implications for continuity from one fiscal year to the next.

Agencies' capabilities to engage in focused evaluation planning and develop well-specified evaluation plans will depend on their ability to develop expertise and sources of information that support that process. This may involve use of outside expertise for advice, including researchers, practitioners, and policy makers. It may also require the capability to conduct or commission preliminary studies to provide input to the process. Such studies might include surveys of programs and policy makers to identify issues and potential sites, feasibility studies to determine if it is likely that certain questions can be answered, and evaluability assessments that examine the readiness and appropriateness of evaluation for candidate programs.

3

When Is an Impact Evaluation Appropriate?

Of the many evaluation questions that might be asked for any criminal justice program, the one that is generally of most interest to policy makers is, "Does it work?" That is, does the program have the intended beneficial effects on the outcomes of interest? Policy makers, for example, might wish to know the effects of a "hot spots" policing program on the rate of violent crime (Braga, 2003) or whether vigorous enforcement of drug laws results in a decrease in drug consumption. As described in the previous chapter, answering these types of questions is the main focus of impact evaluation.

A valid and informative impact evaluation, however, cannot necessarily be conducted for every criminal justice program whose effects are of interest to policy makers. Impact evaluation is inherently difficult and depends upon specialized research designs, data collections, and statistical analysis (discussed in more detail in the next chapter). It simply cannot be carried out effectively unless certain minimum conditions and resources are available no matter how skilled the researchers or insistent the policy makers. Moreover, even under otherwise favorable circumstances, it is rarely possible to obtain credible answers about the effects of a criminal justice program within a short time period or at low cost.

For policy makers and sponsors of impact evaluation research, this situation has a number of significant implications. Most important, it means that to have a reasonable probability of success, impact evaluations should be launched only with careful planning and firm indications that the prerequisite conditions are in place. In the face of the inevitable limited resources for evaluation research, how programs are selected for impact evaluation may also be critical. Broad priorities that spread resources too thinly may reduce the likelihood that any evaluation can be carried out well enough to produce credible and useful results. Focused priorities that concentrate resources in relatively few impact evaluations may be equally unproductive if the program circumstances for those few are not amenable to evaluation.

There are no criteria for determining which programs are most appropriate for impact evaluation that will ensure that every evaluation can be effectively implemented and yield valid findings. Two different kinds of considerations that are generally relevant are developed here—one relating to the practical or political significance of the program and one relating to how amenable it is to evaluation.

SIGNIFICANCE OF THE PROGRAM

Across the full spectrum of criminal justice programs, those that may be appropriate for impact evaluation will not generally be identifiable through any single means or source. Participants in different parts of the system will have different interests and priorities that focus their attention on different programs. Sponsors and funders of programs will often want to know if the programs in which they have made investments have the desired effects. Practitioners may be most interested in evaluations of the programs they currently use and of alternative programs that might be better. Policy makers will be interested in evaluations that help them make resource allocation decisions about the programs they should support. Researchers often focus their attention on innovative program concepts with potential importance for future application.

It follows that adequate identification of programs that may be significant enough to any one of these groups to be candidates for impact evaluation will require input from informed representatives of that group. Sponsors of evaluation research across the spectrum of criminal justice programs will need input from all these groups if they wish to identify the candidates for impact evaluation likely to be most significant for the field.

Two primary mechanisms create programs for which impact evaluation may contribute vital practical information. One mechanism is the evolution of innovative programs or the combination of existing program elements into new programs that have great potential in the eyes of the policy community. Such programs may be developed by researchers or practitioners and fielded rather narrowly. The practice of arresting perpetrators of domestic violence when police were called to the scene began in this fashion (Sherman, 1992). With the second mechanism, programs spring into broad acceptance as a result of grassroots enthusiasm but may lack an empirical or theoretical underpinning. Project DARE, with its use of police officers to provide drug prevention education in schools, followed that path. Programs stemming from both sources are potentially significant, though for different reasons, and it would be shortsighted to focus on one to the exclusion of the other.

Given a slate of candidate programs for which impact evaluation may have significance for the field from the perspective of one concerned group or another, it may still be necessary to set priorities among them. A useful conceptual framework from health intervention research for appraising the significance of an intervention is summarized in the acronym, RE-AIM, for Reach, Effectiveness, Adoption, Implementation, and Maintenance (Glasgow, Vogt, and Boles, 1999). When considering whether a program is a candidate for impact evaluation these elements can be thought of as a chain with the potential value of an evaluation constrained by the weakest link in that chain. These criteria can be used to assess a program's significance and, correspondingly, the value of evaluation results about its effects. We will consider these elements in order.

Reach. Reach is the scope of the population that could potentially benefit from the intervention if it proves effective. Other things equal, an intervention validated by evaluation that is applicable to a larger population has more practical significance than one applicable to a smaller population. Reach may also encompass specialized, hard-to-serve populations for which more general programs may not be suitable. Drug courts, from this perspective, have great reach because of the high prevalence of substance abuse among offenders. A culture-specific program to reduce violence against Native American women, however, would also have reach because there are currently few programs tailored for this population.

Effectiveness. The potential value of a program is, of course, constrained by its effectiveness when it is put into practice. It is the job of impact evaluation to determine effectiveness, which makes this a difficult criterion to apply when selecting programs for impact evaluation. Nonetheless, an informed judgment call about the potential effectiveness of a program can be important for setting evaluation priorities. For some programs, there may be preliminary evidence of efficacy or effectiveness that can inform judgment. Consistency with well-established theory and the clinical judgment of experienced practitioners may also be useful touchstones. The positive effects of cognitive-behavioral therapies demonstrated for a range of mental health problems, for instance, supports the expectation that they might also be effective for sex offenders.

Adoption. Adoption is the potential market for a program. Adoption is a complex constellation of ideology, politics, and bureaucratic preferences that is influenced by intellectual fashion and larger social forces as well as rational assessment of the utility of a program. Given equal effectiveness and ease of implementation, some programs will be less attractive and acceptable to potential users than others. The assessment of those factors by potential adopters can thus provide valuable information for prioritizing programs for impact evaluation. The widespread adoption of bootcamps during the 1990s, for instance, indicated that this type of paramilitary program had considerable political and social appeal and was compatible with the program concepts held by criminal justice practitioners.

Implementation. Some programs are more difficult to implement than others, and for some it may be more difficult to sustain the quality of the service delivery in ongoing practice. Other things equal, a program that is straightforward to implement and sustain is more valuable than a program that requires a great deal of effort and monitoring to yield its full potential. Mentoring programs as a delinquency prevention strategy for at-risk juveniles, for instance, are generally easier and less costly to implement than family counseling programs with their requirements for highly trained personnel and regular meetings with multiple family members.

Maintenance. Maintenance, in this context, refers to the maintenance of positive program effects over time. The more durable the effect of a program, the greater is its value as a beneficial social intervention. For instance, if improved street lighting reduces street crimes by making high crime areas more visible (Farrington and Welsh, 2002), the effects are not likely to diminish significantly as long as criminals prefer to conduct their business away from public view.

Making good judgments on such criteria in advance of an impact evaluation will rarely be an easy task and will almost always have to be done on the basis of insufficient information. To assess the potential significance of a criminal justice program and, hence, the potential significance of an impact evaluation of that program, however, requires some such assessment. Because it is a difficult task, expert criminal justice professionals, policy makers, and researchers should be employed to review candidate programs, discuss their significance for impact evaluation, and make recommendations about the corresponding priorities.

EVALUABILITY OF THE PROGRAM

A criminal justice program that is significant in terms of the criteria described above may, nonetheless, be inappropriate for impact evaluation. The nature of the program and its circumstances, the prerequisites for credible research, or the available resources may fall short of what is required to conduct an adequate assessment of program effects. This is an unfortunate circumstance, but one that must be recognized in any process of decision making about where to invest resources for impact evaluation. The number of impact evaluations found to be inadequately implemented in the GAO reports reviewed in Chapter 1 of this report is evidence of the magnitude of the potential difficulties in completing even well-designed projects of this sort.

At issue is the *evaluability* of a program—whether the conceptualization, configuration, and situation of a program make it amenable to evaluation research and, if so, what would be required to conduct the research. Ultimately, effective impact evaluation depends on four basic preconditions: (a) a sufficiently developed and documented program to be evaluated, (b) the ability to obtain relevant and reliable data on the program outcomes of interest, (c) a research design capable of distinguishing program effects from other influences on the outcomes, and (d) sufficient resources to adequately conduct the research. Item (c), relating to research design for impact evaluation, poses considerable technical and practical challenges and, additionally, must be tailored rather specifically to the circumstances of the program being evaluated. It is discussed in the next chapter of this report. The other preconditions for effective impact evaluation are somewhat more general and are reviewed below.

The Program

At the most basic level, impact evaluation is most informative when there is a well-defined program to evaluate. Finding effects is of little value if it is not possible to specify what was done to bring about those effects, that is, the program's theory of change and the way it is operationalized. Such a program cannot be replicated nor easily used by other practitioners who wish to adopt it. Moreover, before beginning a study, researchers should be able to identify the effects, positive and negative, that the program might plausibly produce and know what target population or social conditions are expected to show those effects.

Programs can be poorly defined in several different ways that will create difficulties for impact evaluation. One is simply that the intended program activities and services are not documented, though they may be well-structured in practice. It is commonplace for many medical and mental health programs to develop treatment protocols—manuals that describe what the treatment is and how it is to be delivered—but this is not generally the case for criminal justice programs. In such instances, the evaluation research may need to include an observational and descriptive component to characterize the nature of the program under consideration. As mentioned in Chapter 2, a process evaluation to determine how well the program is implemented and how completely and adequately it delivers the intended services is also frequently conducted along with an impact evaluation. These procedures allow any findings about program effects to be accompanied by a description of the program as actually delivered as well as of the program as intended.

Another variant on the issue of program definition occurs for programs that provide significantly different services to different program participants, whether inadvertently or by intent. A juvenile diversion project, for instance, may prescribe quite different services for different first offenders based on a needs assessment. A question about the impact of this diversion program may be answered in terms of the average effect on recidivism across the variously treated juveniles served. The mix of services provided to each juvenile and the basis for deciding on that mix, however, may be critical to any success the program shows. If those aspects are not well-defined in the program procedures, it can be challenging for the evaluation to fully specify these key features in a way that adequately describes the program or permits replication and emulation elsewhere.

One of the more challenging situations for impact evaluation is a multisite program with substantial variation across sites in how the program is configured and implemented (Herrell and Straw, 2002). Consider, for example, a program that provides grants to communities to better coordinate the law enforcement, prosecutorial, and judicial response to domestic violence through more vigorous enforcement of existing laws. The activities developed at each site to accomplish this purpose may be quite different, as well as the mix of criminal justice participants, the roles designated for them in the program, and the specific laws selected for emphasis. Arguably under such circumstances each site has implemented a different program and each would require its own impact evaluation. A national evaluation that attempts to encompass the whole program has the challenge of sampling sites in a representative manner but, even then, is largely restricted to examining the average effects across these rather different program implementations. With sufficient specification of the program variants and separate effects at each site, more differentiated findings about impact could be developed, but at what may be greatly increased cost.

Outcome Data

Impact evaluation requires data describing key outcomes, whether drawn from existing sources or collected as part of the evaluation. The most important outcome data are those that relate to the most policy-relevant outcomes, e.g., crime reduction. Even when we observe relevant outcomes, there may be important trade-offs between the sensitivity and scope of the measure. For example, when evaluating the minimum drinking age laws, Cook and Tauchen (1984) considered whether to use "fatal nighttime single-vehicle accidents" (which has a high percentage of alcohol-related cases, making it sensitive to an alcohol-oriented intervention) or an overall measure of highway fatalities (which should capture the full effect of the law, but is less sensitive to small changes). In some instances, the only practical measures may be for intermediate outcomes presumed to lead to the ultimate outcome (e.g., improved conflict-resolution skills for a violence prevention program or drug consumption during the last month rather than lifetime consumption). There are several basic features that should be considered when assessing the adequacy and availability of outcome data for an impact evaluation. In particular, the quality of the evaluation will depend, in part, on the representativeness, accuracy, and accessibility of the relevant data (NRC, 2004).

Representativeness

A fundamental requirement for outcome data is that they represent the population addressed by the program. The standard scheme for accomplishing this when conducting an impact evaluation is to select the research participants with a random sample from the target population, but other well-defined sampling schemes can also be used in some instances. For example, case-control or response-based sampling designs can be useful for studying rare events. To investigate factors associated with homicide, a case-control design might select as cases those persons who have been murdered, and then select as controls a number of subjects from the same population with similar characteristics who were not murdered. If random sampling or another representative selection is not feasible given the circumstances of the program to be evaluated, the outcome data, by definition, will not characterize the outcomes for the actual target population served by the program. Similar considerations apply when the outcome data are collected from existing records or data archives. Many of the data sets used to study criminal justice policy are not probability samples from the particular populations at which the policy may be aimed (see NRC, 2001). The National Crime Victimization Survey (NCVS), for example, records information on nonfatal incidents of crime victims but does not survey offenders. Household-based surveys such as the NCVS and the General Social Survey (GSS) are limited to the population of persons with stable residences, thereby omitting transients and other persons at high risk for crime and violence. The GSS is representative of the United States and the nine census regions, but it is too sparse geographically to support conclusions at the finer levels of geographical aggregation where the target populations for many criminal justice programs will be found.

Accuracy

The accuracy of the outcome data available is also an important consideration for an impact evaluation. The validity of outcome data is compromised when the measures do not adequately represent the behaviors or events the program is intended to affect, as when perpetrators understate the frequency of their criminal behavior in self-report surveys. The reliability of the data suffers when unsystematic errors are reflected in the outcome measures, as when arrest records are incomplete. The bias and noise associated with outcome data with poor validity or reliability can easily be great enough to distort or mask program effects. Thus credible impact evaluation cannot be conducted with outcome data lacking sufficient accuracy in either of these ways.

Accessibility

If the necessary outcome data are not accessible to the researcher, it will obviously not be possible to conduct an impact evaluation. Data on individuals' criminal offense records that are kept in various local or regional archives, for instance, are usually not accessible to researchers without a court order or analogous legal authorization. If the relevant authorities are unwilling to provide that authorization, those records become unavailable as a source of outcome data. The programs being evaluated may themselves have outcome data that they are not willing to provide to the evaluator, perhaps for ethical reasons (e.g., victimization reported to counselors) or because they view it as proprietary. In addition, researchers may find that increasingly stringent Institutional Review Board (IRB) standards preclude them from using certain sources of data that may be available (Brainard, 2001; Oakes, 2002). Relevant data collected and archived in existing databases may also be unavailable even when collected with public funding (e.g., Monitoring the Future; NRC, 2001).

Still another form of inaccessible data is encountered when nonresponse rates are likely to be high for an outcome measure, e.g., when a significant portion of the sampled individuals decline to respond at all or fail to answer one or more questions. Nonresponse is an endemic problem in self-report surveys and is especially high with disadvantaged, threatened, deviant, or mobile populations of the sort that are often involved in criminal justice programs. An example from the report on illicit drug policy (NRC, 2001:95-96) illustrates the problem:

Suppose that 100 individuals are asked whether they used illegal drugs during the past year. Suppose that 25 do not respond, so the nonresponse rate is 25 percent. Suppose that 19 of the 75 respondents used illegal drugs during the past year and that the others did not. Then the reported prevalence of illegal drug use is 19/75 = 25.3 percent. However, true prevalence among the 100 surveyed individuals depends on how many of the nonrespondents used illegal drugs. If none did, then true prevalence is 19/100 = 19 percent. If all did, then true prevalence is [(19 + 25)/100] = 44 percent. If between 0 and 25 nonrespondents used illegal drugs, then true prevalence is between 19 and 44 percent. Thus, in this example, nonresponse causes true prevalence to be uncertain within a range of 25 percent.

Resources

The ability to conduct an adequate impact evaluation of a criminal justice program will clearly depend on the availability of resources. Relevant resources include direct funding as a major component, but also encompass a range of nonmonetary considerations. The time available for the evaluation, for instance, is an important resource. Impact evaluations not only require that specialized research designs be implemented but that outcomes for relatively large numbers of individuals (or other affected units) be tracked long enough to determine program effects. Similarly, the availability of expertise related to the demanding technical aspects of impact evaluation research, cooperation from the program to be evaluated, and access to relevant data that has already been collected are important resources for impact evaluation.

The need for these various resources for an impact evaluation is a function of the program's structure and circumstances and the evaluation methods to be used. For example, evaluations of community-based programs, with the community as the unit of analysis, will require participation by a relatively large numbers of communities. This situation will make for a difficult and potentially expensive evaluation project. Evaluating a rehabilitation program for offenders in a correctional institution with outcome data drawn from administrative records, on the other hand, might require fewer resources.

SELECTING PROGRAMS APPROPRIATE
FOR IMPACT EVALUATION

No agency or group of agencies that sponsor program evaluation will have the resources to support impact evaluation for every program of potential interest to some relevant party. If the objective is to optimize the practical and policy relevance of the resulting knowledge, programs should be selected for evaluation on the basis of (a) the significance of the program, e.g., the scope of practice and policy likely to be affected and (b) the extent to which the circumstances of the program make it amenable to sound evaluation research.

The procedures for making this selection should not necessarily be the same for both these criteria. Judging the practical importance of a program validated by impact evaluation requires informed opinion from a range of perspectives. The same is true for identifying new program concepts that are ripe for evaluation study. Surveys or expert review procedures that obtain input from criminal justice practitioners, policy makers, advocacy groups, researchers, and the like might be used for this purpose.

With a set of programs judged significant identified, assessment of how amenable they are to sound impact evaluation research is a different matter. The expertise relevant to this judgment resides mainly with evaluation researchers who have extensive field experience conducting impact evaluations of criminal justice programs. This expertise might be marshaled through a separate expert review procedure, but there are inherent limits to that approach if the expert informants have insufficient information about the programs at issue. Trustworthy assessments of program evaluability depend upon rather detailed knowledge of the nature of the program and its services, the target population, the availability of relevant data, and a host of other such matters.

More informed judgments about the likelihood of successful impact evaluation will result if this information is first collected in a relatively systematic manner from the programs under consideration. The procedure for accomplishing this is called *evaluability assessment* (introduced in Chapter 2). The National Institute of Justice has recently begun conducting evaluability assessments as part of its process for selecting programs for impact evaluation. Their procedure[1] involves two stages: an initial screening using administrative records and telephone inquiries plus a site visit to programs that survive the initial screening. The site visit involves observations of the project as well as interviews with key project staff, the project director, and (if appropriate) key partners and members of the target population. Box 3-1 lists some of the factors assessed at each of these stages.

The extent to which the results of such an assessment are informative when considering programs for impact evaluation is illustrated by NIJ's

---

[1]There are actually two different assessment tools —one for local and another for national programs. This description focuses on the local assessment instrument.

experience with this procedure. In the most recent round of evaluability assessments, a pool of approximately 200 earmarked programs was reduced to only eight that were ultimately judged to be good candidates for an impact evaluation that would have a reasonable probability of yielding useful information.

BOX 3-1
Factors Considered in Each Stage of NIJ Evaluability Assessments

Initial Project Screening

- What do we already know about projects like these?
- What could an evaluation of this project add to what we know?
- Which audiences would benefit from this evaluation?
- What could they do with the findings?
- Is the grantee interested in being evaluated?
- What is the background/history of this project?
- At what stage of implementation is it?
- What are the project's outcome goals in the view of the project director?
- Does the proposal/project director describe key project elements?
- Do they describe how the project's primary activities contribute to goals?
- Can you sketch the logic by which activities should affect goals?
- Are there other local projects providing similar services that could be used for comparison?
- Will samples that figure in outcome measurement be large enough to generate statistically significant findings for modest effect sizes?
- Is the grantee planning an evaluation?
- What data systems exist that would facilitate evaluation?
- What are the key data elements contained in these systems?
- Are there data to estimate unit costs of services or activities?
- Are there data about possible comparison samples?
- In general, how useful are the data systems to an impact evaluation?

Site Visit

- Is the project being implemented as advertised?
- What is the intervention to be evaluated?
- What outcomes could be assessed? By what measures?
- Are there valid comparison groups?
- Is random assignment possible?
- What threats to a sound evaluation are most likely to occur?
- Are there hidden strengths in the project?
- What are the sizes and characteristics of the target populations?
- How is the target population identified (i.e., what are eligibility criteria)? Who/what gets excluded as a target?
- Have the characteristics of the target population changed over time?
- How large would target and comparison samples be after one year of observation?
- What would the target population receive in a comparison sample?
- What are the shortcomings/gaps in delivering the intervention?
- What do recipients of the intervention think the project does?
- How do they assess the services received?
- What kinds of data elements are available from existing data sources?
- What specific input, process, and outcome measures would they support?
- How complete are data records? Can you get samples?
- What routine reports are produced?
- Can target populations be followed over time?
- Can services delivered be identified?
- Can systems help diagnose implementation problems?
- Does staff tell consistent stories about the project?
- Are their backgrounds appropriate for the project's activities?
- What do partners provide/receive?
- How integral to project success are the partners?
- What changes is the director willing to make to support the evaluation?

4

How Should an Impact
Evaluation Be Designed?

Assuming that a criminal justice program is evaluable and an impact evaluation is feasible, an appropriate research design must be developed. The basic idea of an impact evaluation is simple. Program outcomes are measured and compared to the outcomes that would have resulted in the absence of the program. In practice, however, it is difficult to design a credible evaluation study in which such a comparison can be made. The fundamental difficulty is that whereas the program being evaluated is operational and its outcomes are observable, at least in principle, the outcomes in the absence of the program are counterfactual and not observable. This situation requires that the design provide some basis for constructing a credible estimate of the outcomes for the counterfactual conditions.

Another fundamental characteristic of impact evaluation is that the design must be tailored to the circumstances of the particular program being evaluated, the nature of its target population, the outcomes of interest, the data available, and the constraints on collecting new data. As a result, it is difficult to define a "best" design for impact evaluation a priori. Rather, the issue is one of determining the best design for a particular program under the particular conditions presented to the researcher when the evaluation is undertaken. This feature of impact evaluation has significant implications for how such research should be designed and also for how the quality of the design should be evaluated.

THE REPERTOIRE OF RELEVANT RESEARCH DESIGNS

Establishing credible estimates of what the outcomes would have been without the program, all else equal, is the most demanding part of impact evaluation, but also the most critical. When those estimates are convincing, the effects found in the evaluation can be attributed to the program rather than to any of the many other possible influences on the outcome variables. In this case, the evaluation is considered to have high *internal validity*. For example, a simple comparison of recidivism rates for those sentenced to prison and those not sentenced would have low internal validity for estimating the effect of prison on reoffending. Any differences in recidivism outcomes could easily be due to preexisting differences between the groups. Judges are more likely to sentence offenders to prison who have serious prior records. Prisoners' greater recidivism rates may not be the result of their prison experience but, rather, the fact that they are more serious offenders in the first place. The job of a good impact evaluation design is to neutralize or rule out such threats to the internal validity of a study.

Although numerous research designs are used to assess program effects, it is useful to classify them into three broad categories: randomized experiments, quasi-experiments, and observational designs. Each, under optimal circumstances, can provide a valid answer to the question of whether a program has an effect upon the outcomes of interest. However, these designs differ in the assumptions they make, the nature of the problems that undermine those assumptions, the degree of control the researcher must have over program exposure, the way in which they are implemented, the issues encountered in statistical analysis, and in many other ways as well. As a result, it is difficult to make simplistic generalizations about which is the best method for obtaining a valid estimate of the effect of any given intervention. We return to this issue later but first provide an overview of the nature of each of these types of designs.

RANDOMIZED EXPERIMENTS

In randomized experiments, the units toward which program services are directed (usually people or places) are randomly assigned to receive the program or not (intervention and control conditions, respectively). For example, in the Minneapolis Hot Spots Experiment (Sherman and Weisburd, 1995), 110 crime hot spots were randomly allocated to an experimental condition that received high levels of preventive patrol and a control condition with a lower "business as usual" level of patrol. The researchers found a moderate, statistically significant program effect on crime rates. Because the hot spots were assigned by a chance process that took no account of their individual characteristics, the researchers could assume that there were no systematic differences between them other than the level of policing. The differences found on the outcome measures, therefore, could be convincingly interpreted as intervention effects.

The main threat to the internal validity of the randomized experiment is attrition prior to outcome measurement that degrades the randomized groups. In the randomized experiment reported by Berk (2003), offenders were randomly assigned to one of several correctional facilities that used different inmate classification systems. The internal validity of this study would have been compromised if a relatively large proportion of those offenders then left those facilities too quickly to establish the misconduct records that provided the outcome measures, e.g., through unexpected early release or transfers to other facilities. Such attrition cannot automatically be assumed to be random nor unrelated to the characteristics of the respective facilities, thus it degrades the statistical equivalence between the groups that was established by the initial randomization. In the prison settings studied by Berk, low rates of attrition were achieved, but this is not always the case. In many randomized experiments conducted in criminal justice research, attrition is a significant problem.

QUASI-EXPERIMENTS

Quasi-experiments are approximations to randomized experiments that compare selected cases receiving an intervention with selected cases not receiving it, but without random assignment to those conditions (Cook and Campbell, 1979). Quasi-experiments generally fall into three classes. In the most common type, an intervention group is compared with a control group that has been selected on the basis of similarity to the intervention group, a specific selection variable, or perhaps simply convenience. For example, researchers might compare offenders receiving intensive probation supervision with offenders receiving regular probation supervision that is matched on prior offense history, gender, and age. The design of this type that is least vulnerable to internal validity threats is the regression-discontinuity or cutting-point design (Shadish, Cook, and Campbell, 2002). In this design, assignment to intervention and control conditions is made on the basis of scores on an initial measure, e.g., a pretest or risk variable. For example, drug offenders might be assigned to probation if their score on a risk assessment was below a set cut point and to drug court if it was above that cut point. The effects of drug court on subsequent substance use will appear as a discontinuity in the statistical relationship between the risk score and the substance use outcome variable.

A second type of quasi-experiment is the time-series design. This design uses a series of observations on the outcome measure made before the program begins that is then compared with another series made afterward. Thus, researchers might compare traffic accidents per month for the year before a speeding crackdown and the year afterward. Because of the requirement for repeated measures prior to the onset of the intervention, time-series designs are most often used when the outcome variables of interest are available from data archives or public records. The third type of quasi-experiment combines nonrandomized comparison groups with time-series observations, contrasting time series for conditions with and without the program. In this design the researcher might compare traffic accidents before and after a speeding crackdown with comparable time-series data from a similar area in which there was no crackdown. This kind of comparison is sometimes referred to as the difference-in-difference method since the pre-post differences in outcomes for the intervention conditions are compared to the pre-post differences in the comparison condition. Ludwig and Cook (2000), for instance, evaluated the impact of the 1994 Brady act by comparing homicide and suicide rates from 1985 to 1997 in 32 states directly affected by the act with those in 19 states that had equivalent legislation already in place.

Quasi-experimental designs are more vulnerable than randomized designs to influences from sources other than the program that can bias the estimates of effects. The better versions of these designs attempt to statistically account for such extraneous influences. To do that, however, requires that the influences be recognized and understood and that data relevant to dealing with them statistically be available. The greatest threat to the internal validity of quasi-experimental designs, therefore, is usually uncontrolled extraneous influences that have differential effects on the outcome variables that are confounded with the true program effects. Simply stated, the equivalence that one can assume from random allocation of subjects into intervention and control conditions cannot be assumed when allocation into groups is not random. Moreover, these designs, like experimental designs, are vulnerable to attrition after the intervention has begun.

OBSERVATIONAL DESIGNS

The third type of design used for evaluation of crime and justice programs is an observational design. Strictly speaking, all quasi-experiments are observational designs, but we will use this category to differentiate studies that observe natural variation in exposure to the program and model its relationship to variation in the outcome measures with other influences statistically controlled. For example, Ayres and Levitt (1998) examined the effects of Lojack, a device used to retrieve stolen vehicles, on city auto theft rates. They drew their data from official records in cities that varied in the prevalence of Lojack users. Because many factors besides use of Lojack influence auto theft, they attempted to account for these potential threats to validity by controlling for them in a statistical model. This type of structural model has been used to study the effects of law enforcement on cocaine consumption (Rydell and Everingham, 1994), racial discrimination in policing (Todd, 2003), and other criminal justice interventions.

The major threat to the internal validity of observational designs used for impact evaluation is failure to adequately model the processes influencing variation in the program and the outcomes. This problem is of particular concern in criminal justice evaluations because theoretical development in criminology is less advanced than in disciplines, like economics, that rely heavily on observational modeling (Weisburd, 2003). Observational methods require that the researcher have sufficient understanding of the processes underlying intervention outcomes, and the other influences on those outcomes, to develop an adequate statistical model. Concern about the validity of the strong assumptions often needed to identify intervention effects with such modeling approaches has led to the development of methods for imposing weak assumptions that yield bounds on the estimates of the program effect (Manski, 1995; Manski and Nagin, 1998). An example of this technique is presented below.

Manski and Nagin (1998) illustrated the use of bounding methods in observational models in a study of the impact of sentencing options on the recidivism of juvenile offenders. Exploiting the rich data on juvenile offenders collected by the state of Utah, they assessed the two main sentencing options available to judges: residential and nonresidential sentences. Although offenders sentenced to residential treatment are more likely to recidivate, this association may only reflect the tendency of judges to sentence different types of offenders to residential placements than to non-residential ones.

Several sets of findings clearly revealed how conclusions about sentencing policy vary depending on the assumptions made. Two alternative models of judicial decisions were considered. The *outcome optimization* model assumes that judges make sentencing decisions that minimize the chance of recidivism. The *skimming* model assumes that judges sentence high-risk offenders to residential confinement.

In the worst-case analysis where nothing was assumed about sentencing rules or outcomes, only weak conclusions could be drawn about the recidivism implications of the two sentencing options. However, much stronger conclusions were drawn under the judicial decision-making model. If one believes that judges optimize outcomes—that is, choose sentences in an effort to minimize recidivism—the empirical results indicate that residential confinement increases recidivism. If one believes that judges skim—that is, assign high-risk offenders to residential treatment—the results suggest the opposite conclusion, namely that residential confinement reduces recidivism.

SELECTING THE DESIGN FOR AN IMPACT EVALUATION

Because high internal validity can be gained in a well-implemented randomized experiment, it is viewed by many researchers as the best method for impact evaluation (Shadish, Cook, and Campbell, 2002). This is also why randomized designs are generally ranked at the top of a hierarchy of designs in crime and justice reviews of "what works" (e.g., Sherman et al., 2002) and why they have been referred to as the "gold standard" for establishing the effects of interventions in fields such as medicine, public health, and psychology. For the evaluation of criminal justice programs, randomized designs have a long history but, nonetheless, have been used much less frequently than observational and quasi-experimental designs.

Whether a hierarchy of methods with randomized designs at the pinnacle should be defined at the outset for evaluation in criminal justice, however, is a contentious issue. The different views on this point do not derive so much from disagreements on the basic properties of the various designs as from different assessments of the trade-offs associated with their application. Different designs are more or less difficult to implement well in different situations and may provide different kinds of information about program effects.

Well-implemented randomized experiments can be expected to yield results with more certain internal validity than quasi-experimental and observational studies. However, randomized experiments require that the program environment be subject to a certain amount of control by the researcher. This may not be permitted in all sites and, as a result, randomized designs are often implemented in selected sites and situations that may not be representative of the full scope of the program being evaluated. In some cases, randomization is not acceptable for political or ethical reasons. There is, for instance, little prospect of random allocation of sentences for serious offenders or legislative actions such as imposition of the death penalty. Randomized designs are also most easily applied to programs that provide services to units such as individuals or groups that are small enough to be assigned in adequate numbers to experimental conditions. For programs implemented in places or jurisdictions rather than with individuals or groups, assigning sufficient numbers of these larger units to experimental conditions may not be feasible. This is not always the case, however. Wagenaar (1999), for instance, randomly assigned 15 midwestern communities to either a community organizing initiative aimed at changing policies and practices related to youth alcohol access or a control condition.

The advantages of randomized designs are such that it is quite justifiable to favor them for impact evaluation when they are appropriate to the questions at issue and there is a reasonable prospect that they can be implemented well enough to provide credible and useful answers to those questions. In situations where they are not, or cannot, be implemented well, however, they may not be the best choice (Eck, 2002; Pawson and Tilley, 1997) and another design may be more appropriate.

Quasi-experimental and observational designs have particular advantages for investigating program effects in realistic situations and for estimating the effects of other influences on outcomes relative to those produced by the program. For example, the influence of a drug treatment program on drug use may be compared to the effects of marital status or employment. Observational studies are generally less expensive per respondent (Garner and Visher, 2003) and do not require manipulation of experimental conditions. They thus may be able to use larger and more representative samples of the respective target population than those used in randomized designs. Observational studies, therefore, often have strong external validity. When they can also demonstrate good internal validity through plausible modeling assumptions and convincing statistical controls, they have distinct advantages for many evaluation situations. For some situations, such as evaluation of the effects of large-scale policy changes, they are often the only feasible alternative. In criminal justice, however, essential data are often not available and theory is often underdeveloped, which limits the utility of quasi-experimental and observational designs for evaluation purposes.

As this discussion suggests, the choice of a research design for impact evaluation is a complex one that must be based in each case on a careful assessment of the program circumstances, the evaluation questions at issue, practical constraints on the implementation of the research, and the degree to which the assumptions and data requirements of any design can be met. There are often many factors to be weighed in this choice and there are always trade-offs associated with the selection of any approach to conducting an impact evaluation in the real world of criminal justice programs. These circumstances require careful deliberation about which evaluation design is likely to yield the most useful and relevant information for a given situation rather than generalizations about the relative superiority of one method over another. The best guidance, therefore, is not an a priori hierarchy of presumptively better and worse designs, but a process of thoughtful deliberation by knowledgeable and methodologically sophisticated evaluation researchers that takes into account the particulars of the situation and the resources available.

GENERALIZABILITY OF RESULTS

As mentioned in the discussion above, one important aspect of an impact evaluation design may be the extent to which the results can be generalized beyond the particular cases and circumstances actually investigated in the study. *External validity* is concerned with the extent to which such generalizations are defensible. The highest levels of external validity are gained by selecting the units that will participate in the research on the basis of probability samples from the population of such units. For example, in studies of sentencing behavior, the researcher may select cases randomly from a database of all offenders who were convicted during a given period. Often in criminal justice evaluations, all available cases are examined for a specific period of time. In the Inmate Classification Experiment conducted by Berk (2003), 20,000 inmates admitted during a six-month period were randomly assigned to an innovative or traditional classification system.

There are often substantial difficulties in defining the target population, either because a complete census of its members is unavailable or because the specific members are unknown. For example, in the Multidimensional Treatment Foster Care study mentioned above, the researchers could not identify the population of juveniles eligible for foster care but rather drew their sample from youth awaiting placement. The researchers might reasonably assume that those youth are representative of the broader population, but they cannot be sure that the particular group selected during that particular study period is not different in some important way. To the extent that the researcher cannot assure that each member of a population has a known probability of being selected for the research sample used in the impact evaluation, external validity is threatened.

Considerations of external validity also apply to the sites in a multisite program. When criminal justice evaluations are limited to specific sites, they may or may not be representative of the population of sites in which the program is, or could be, implemented. Berk's (2003) study of a prison classification system assessed impact at several correctional facilities in California, but not all of them. The representativeness of the sites studied will depend on how they are selected and can be assured only if they are a random sample of the whole population of sites. It is important not to confuse the level at which an inference can be made; for example, a researcher may select a sample of subjects from a single prison but interpret the results as if they generalized to the population of prisons. In the absence of additional information, the only strictly valid statistical generalization is to the prisoners from which the subject sample was drawn. An assumption that the program would work equally well in a prison with different characteristics and a different offender population may be questionable.

STATISTICAL POWER

Another important design consideration for impact evaluations is statistical power, that is, the ability of the research design to detect a program effect of a given magnitude at a stipulated level of statistical significance. If a study has low statistical power it means that it is likely to lead to a statistically nonsignificant finding even if there is a meaningful program impact. Such studies are "designed for failure"—an effective program has no reasonable chance of showing a statistically significant effect.

Statistical power is a function of the nature and number of units on which outcome data are collected (sample size), as well as the variability and measurement of the data and the magnitude of the program effect (if any) to be detected. It is common for criminal justice evaluations to ignore statistical power and equally common for them to lack adequate power to provide a sensitive test of the effectiveness of the treatments they evaluate (Brown, 1989; Weisburd, Petrosino, and Mason, 1993). An underpowered evaluation that does not find significant program effects cannot be correctly interpreted as a failure of the program, though that is often the conclusion implied (Weisburd, Lum, and Yang, 2003). For example, if a randomized experiment included only 30 cases each for the intervention and control conditions, and the effect of the intervention was a .40 recidivism rate for the intervention group compared to .65 for the control group, the likelihood that it would be found statistically significant at the $p < .05$ level in any one study is only about 50 percent though it is rather clearly a large effect in practical terms.

Even when statistical power is examined in criminal justice evaluations, the approach is frequently superficial. For example, it is common for criminal justice evaluators to estimate statistical power for program effects defined as "moderate" in size on the basis of Cohen's (1988) general suggestions. Effect sizes in crime and justice are often much smaller than that, but this does not mean that they do not have practical significance (Lipsey, 2000). In the recidivism example used above, a "small" effect size as defined by Cohen would correspond to the difference between a .40 recidivism rate for the intervention group and .50 for the control group. A reduction of this magnitude for a large criminal population, however, would produce a very large societal benefit. It is important for evaluators to define at the outset the effect that is meaningful for the specific program and outcome that is examined.

The design components of a study are often interrelated so that manipulation of one component to increase statistical power may adversely affect another component. In a review of criminal justice experiments in sanctions, Weisburd et al. (1993) found that increasing sample size (which is the most common method for increasing statistical power) often affects the intensity of dosage in a study or the heterogeneity of the participants examined. For example, in the RAND Intensive Probation experiments (Petersilia and Turner, 1993), the researchers relaxed admissions requirements to the program in order to gain more cases. This led to the inclusion of participants who were less likely to be affected by the treatment, and thus made it more difficult to identify a treatment impact. Accordingly, estimation of statistical power like other decisions that a researcher makes in designing a project must be made in the context of the specific program and practices examined.

AVOIDING THE BLACK BOX OF TREATMENT

Whether a program succeeds or fails in producing the intended effects, it is important to policy makers and practitioners to know exactly what the program was that had those outcomes. Many criminal justice evaluations suffer from the "black box" problem—a great deal of attention is given to the description of the outcome but little is directed toward describing the nature of the program. For example, in the Kansas City Preventive Patrol Experiment (Kelling et al., 1974), there was no direct measure of the amount of patrol actually present in the three treatment areas. Accordingly, there was no objective way to determine how the conditions actually differed. It is thus important that a careful process evaluation accompany an impact evaluation to provide descriptive information on what happened during a study. Process evaluations should include both qualitative and quantitative information to provide a full picture of the program. If the evaluation then finds a significant effect, it will be possible to clearly describe what produced it. Such description is essential if a program is to be replicated at other sites or implemented more broadly. If the evaluation does not find an effect (as in Kansas City), the researcher is able to examine whether this was the result of a theory failure or an implementation failure.

THE LIMITATIONS OF SINGLE STUDIES

It is not uncommon in criminal justice to draw broad policy conclusions from a single study conducted at one site. The outcomes of such a study, however, may have more to do with the particular characteristics of the agency or personnel involved than with the strengths or weaknesses of the program itself. Note, for example, the variation Braga (2003) found in the effects of hot spots policing across five randomized control group studies. Similarly, a strong program impact in one jurisdiction may not carry over to others that have offenders or victims drawn from different ethnic communities or socioeconomic backgrounds (Berk, 1992; Sherman, 1992). This does not mean that single-site studies cannot be useful for drawing conclusions about program effects or developing policy, only that caution must be used to avoid overgeneralizing their significance.

Such circumstances highlight the importance of conducting multiple studies and integrating their findings so that meaningful conclusions can be drawn. The most common technique for integrating results from impact evaluation studies is meta-analysis or systematic review (Cooper, 1998). Meta-analysis allows the pooling of multiple studies in a specific area of interest into a single analysis in which each study is an independent observation. The main advantage of meta-analysis over traditional narrative reviews is that it yields an estimate of the average size of the intervention effect over a large number of studies while also allowing analysis of the sources of variation across studies in those effects (Cooper and Hedges, 1994; Lipsey and Wilson, 2001).

Another approach for overcoming the inherent weakness of single-site studies is replication research. In this case, studies are replicated at multiple sites within a broader program of study initiated by a funding agency. The Spouse Assault Replication Program (Garner, Fagan, and Maxwell, 1995) of the National Institute of Justice is an example of this approach. In that study, as in other replication studies, it has been difficult to combine investigations into a single statistical analysis (e.g., Petersilia and Turner, 1993), and it is common for replication studies to be discussed in ways similar to narrative reviews. A more promising approach, the multicenter clinical trial, is common in medical studies but is rare in criminal justice evaluations (Fleiss, 1982; Stanley, Stjernsward, and Isley, 1981). In multicenter clinical trials, a single study is conducted under very strict controls across a sample of sites. Although multicenter trials are rare in criminal justice evaluations, Weisburd and Taxman (2000) described the design of one such trial that involved innovative drug treatments. In this case a series of centers worked together to develop a common set of treatments and common protocols for measuring outcomes. The multicenter approach enhances external validity by supporting inferences not only to the respondent samples at each site, but also to the more general population that the sites represent collectively.

5

How Should the
Evaluation Be Implemented?

Many of the problems that result in unsuccessful impact evaluations come about because the evaluation plan was not carried
out as intended, not because the evaluation was poorly designed. Some of the more common areas in which study designs break
down in implementation are:

• failure to obtain the necessary number of cases to construct treatment and control groups and/or attain sufficient statistical power;
• failure to acquire a suitable comparison group in quasi-experimental studies;
• attrition, especially when it affects the treatment and control groups
differently;
• dilution of the service delivery that weakens the program being
tested; and
• failure to identify essential covariates or obtain measures of them
in observational studies.

Problems such as these undermine the validity of the conclusions an
impact evaluation can support and, if serious, can keep the study from
being completed in any useful form. This section describes procedures
that can reduce the likelihood of implementation problems and determine
when an evaluation that is not likely to yield useful results should be
aborted. The discussion is divided into subsections for actions that can be
taken prior to awarding and during the evaluation contract. The common
theme across these subsections is that forethought, careful planning, and

informed monitoring can minimize problems associated with the implementation of an impact evaluation.

STEPS THAT CAN BE TAKEN PRIOR TO AWARDING THE EVALUATION CONTRACT

Developing an Effective Request for Proposals (RFP)

As noted in Chapter 2, an initial step for ensuring a high-quality evaluation is a well-developed account of the questions that need to be answered and the form such answers should take to be useful to the intended audience. These considerations, in turn, have rather direct implications for the design and implementation of an impact evaluation. The usual vehicle for translating this critical background information into guidelines and expectations for the evaluation design and implementation is a Request for Proposal (RFP) circulated to potential evaluators. An RFP that is based on solid information about the nature and circumstances of the program to be evaluated should encourage prospective evaluators to plan for the likely implementation problems. For instance, a thorough RFP might prompt the applicant to provide (a) a power analysis to support the proposed number of cases; (b) evidence that supports the claim that a sufficient number of cases will be available (e.g., pilot study results or analysis of agency data showing that the number of cases that fit the selection criteria were available in a recent period); (c) a carefully considered plan for actually obtaining the necessary number of cases; and (d) a management plan for overseeing and correcting, if necessary, the process of recruitment of cases for the study.

When such background information is not provided in the RFP, it will fall to the evaluation contractor to discover it and adapt the evaluation plans accordingly. In such circumstances, the RFP and the terms of the evaluation contract must allow such flexibility. In addition, consideration must be given to the possibility that the discovery process will reveal circumstances that make successful implementation of the evaluation unlikely. Where there is significant uncertainty about the feasibility of an impact evaluation, a two-step contracting process would be advisable, with the first step focusing on developing background information and formulating the evaluation plan and the second step, if warranted, being the implementation of that plan and completion of the evaluation.

Funding agencies and evaluators have used a number of approaches to developing the information needed to formulate an instructive RFP or planning the evaluation directly. Site visits, for example, are one common way to assess whether essential resources such as space, equipment, and staff will be available to the evaluation project and to ensure that key local partners are on board. An especially probing version of a site visit is a structured evaluability assessment of the sort described in Chapter 2. The distinctive function of an evaluability assessment is to focus specifically on questions critical to determining if a program is appropriate for impact evaluation and how such an evaluation would be feasible (Wholey, 1994). Prior process evaluations, as described in earlier chapters, may also provide detailed program information useful for developing an RFP and planning the impact evaluation.

When there are questions about the availability of a sufficient number of participants to meet the requirements of an evaluation study, a "pipeline" analysis may be appropriate (Shadish, Cook, and Campbell, 2002). Pipeline studies are conducted prior to the actual evaluation as a pilot test of the specific procedures for identifying the cases that will be selected for an evaluation according to the planned eligibility criteria. They address the unfortunately common situation in which what appears to be an ample number of potential participants in the evaluation sharply diminishes when the actual selection is made. An illustration of the need for a pipeline analysis is presented in Box 5-1.

Similarly, pilot or feasibility studies can test important procedures such as randomization and consent, for example, to determine what effects they may have on sample attrition. A preliminary study of this sort also provides an opportunity to discover other aspects of the program circumstances that may present problems or have implications for how the evaluation is designed. The evaluation reported by Berk (2003) of a prison classification scheme and that reported by Chamberlain (2003) of Multidimensional Treatment Foster Care for delinquents, for instance, both built on preliminary studies conducted before the main evaluation. For complex evaluations, a design advisory group consisting of experts in evaluation methodology and study design might be funded to assist in developing an evaluation plan that is informed by the findings from whatever preliminary studies have been conducted.

Development of the RFP and interpretation of available information about the program circumstances must also consider issues related to how the evaluation is organized. Common models include configuration of the evaluation through one or more local evaluation teams, a national evaluator working directly with the local site(s), or a national evaluator working with local teams. Local evaluation teams have the advantage of proximity and the opportunity to develop close working relationships with the program, factors that facilitate implementation of the evaluation plan and effective quality control monitoring. However, they are not always able to marshal the level of expertise and experience available to a national team and, in multisite evaluations, obtaining comparable designs and outcome data across different local teams is often difficult. Prelimi-

---

BOX 5-1
Pipeline Analyses and Pilot Testing

A recent randomized trial funded by the National Institute on Drug Abuse testing the effects of the Strengthening Families Program for reducing drug use and antisocial behavior in a large, urban population encountered major challenges with recruitment and retention of participants (Gottfredson et al., 2004). Of 1,403 families recruited, only 1,036 registered and, of those, only 715 showed up to complete the pretest. Then, only 68 percent of these pretested families who had been randomly assigned to the intervention attended at least one session of the program. Although the research plan anticipated some attrition, the actual rate was much higher. In this instance, a pipeline analysis that conducted preliminary focused assessments of the likely yield at each step of the process would have helped avoid these problems. Surfacing the recruitment and retention problems earlier would then have allowed them to be better anticipated in the evaluation design.

This same study provides an example of how pilot-testing the randomization procedures might reveal problems that could weaken the study design. This evaluation design involved three intervention conditions (equal numbers of sessions of child skills training only, parent skills training only, and parent and child skills training plus family skills training) compared with a minimal treatment control condition. Part way into the study it was discovered that families assigned to the parent skills only condition were significantly less likely to attend the program than families assigned to the other conditions, probably because they thought that their children, rather than themselves, needed the help. This differential attendance potentially compromised the comparison across conditions because any difference favoring the child-only and family conditions might have been attributed to the greater number of contact hours rather than the content of the program.

A preliminary year of funding for piloting study procedures and conducting pipeline analyses would have strengthened this study by alerting the investigators to the challenges so that they could refine the procedures before the study began.

---

nary investigations and input from an advisory panel that attends directly to the question of how best to organize the evaluation may be especially important for large multisite projects.

Site visits, evaluability assessments, pipeline analyses, and other such preliminary investigations, of course, add to the cost of an evaluation and are often used, if at all, only for large projects. Those costs, however, must be balanced against the potentially greater cost of funding an evaluation that ultimately fails to be implemented well enough to produce useful results. Preliminary studies cannot ensure that problems will not arise during the course of the actual evaluation project. Nonetheless, they do help surface some of the potentially more serious problems so they can be handled beforehand or a decision made about whether to go ahead with the evaluation.

Reviewing Evaluation Proposals

Knowledgeable reviewers can contribute not only to the selection of sound evaluation proposals but also to improving the methodological quality and potential for successful implementation of those selected. The comments and suggestions of reviewers experienced in designing and implementing impact evaluations may identify weak areas and needed revision in even the highest scoring evaluation proposals under review. An agency can reduce the likelihood of implementation problems by using these comments and suggestions to require changes in the evaluation design before a grant or contract is awarded.

Obtaining good advice about ways to improve the design and implementation of the most promising evaluation proposals, of course, requires that those reviewing the proposals have relevant expertise. In areas like criminal justice where there are strong conflicting opinions about methods of evaluation, it is critical to develop and maintain balanced review panels. When it is necessary for these panels to deal with proposals involving widely different evaluation methodologies, the reviewers collectively must be broad minded and eclectic enough to make reasoned comparisons of the relative merits of different approaches. One advantage of an agency process that produces RFPs that are well-developed and specific with regard to the relevant questions and preferred design is that review panels can be configured to represent expertise distinctive to the stipulated methods. Under these circumstances, a specialized panel will be more likely to provide advice that will improve the design and implementation plans of the more attractive proposals as well as better judge their initial quality.

Agencies often struggle to design and carry out review processes that meet high standards of scientific quality while maintaining fairness and representation of diverse views. They may, for instance, include practitioners as well as scientific reviewers to ensure that the research funded has policy relevance. Diversity that extends much beyond research expertise in impact evaluation, however, will dilute rather than strengthen the ability of a review panel to select and improve evaluation proposals. This is an especially important consideration if impact evaluations that meet high scientific standards are desired. Practitioners rarely have the training and experience necessary to provide sound judgments on research methods and implementation, though their input may be very helpful for defining agency priorities and identifying significant programs for evaluation. If practitioner views on the policy relevance of specific evaluation proposals are desired, a two-stage review would be the best approach. The policy relevance of the programs under consideration for evaluation would be first judged by knowledgeable policy makers, practitioners, and researchers. Proposals that pass this screen would then receive a scientific review from a panel of well-qualified researchers. The review panels at this second stage could then focus solely on the scientific merit and likelihood of successful implementation of the proposed research.

For purposes of obtaining careful reviews and sound advice for improving proposals, standing review committees rather than ad hoc ones have much to recommend them. The National Institutes of Health (NIH), for example, utilizes standing review committees with a rotating membership. This contrasts with other agencies, such as the National Institute of Justice, whose review committees are composed anew for each competition. A higher level of prestige is often associated with membership on a standing committee, making it more attractive to senior researchers. Members of standing panels also learn from each other and from prior proposals in ways that may improve the quality of their reviews and advice. In addition, standing panels become part of the infrastructure of the agency and develop an institutional memory helpful in maintaining consistency in reviews over time.

Regardless of the form of the review panel, reviewers benefit from structure in the review process. A helpful aid, for instance, is a checklist or code sheet that includes guidelines for the level of rigor expected for different features of the research methods (e.g., basic design, measurement, etc.) and characteristic implementation issues (e.g., adequate samples, availability of data) for different types of studies. Such a list helps ensure thorough and consistent reviews and, if revised to incorporate prior experience, becomes a comprehensive guide to potential shortcomings in the design or implementation plans under consideration. Also, if included in the request for proposal, this list will encourage proposal authors to address the known problem areas and include sufficient detail for the resulting plans to be judged.

Formulating a Management Plan

Although agencies do not always require a detailed list of tasks to be completed by certain dates as part of an evaluation proposal, a clear plan in advance of the award can facilitate later project management. Such a plan could be required as a first step by a contractor or grantee selected to conduct an evaluation project. This plan would spell out specific milestones in the evaluation that must be reached by certain dates in order for the evaluation to proceed on schedule, for example, the successful recruitment of sites, configuration of experimental groups, and enrollment of subjects. A sound management plan would also identify critical benchmarks or events that must occur in order for the project to proceed toward successful implementation, e.g., letters of commitment from crucial local partners.

Written memoranda of understanding (MOUs) with key partners are another strategy that can help keep a project on track during the implementation phase. Such MOUs might be required with all critical partners who have committed important resources (such as personnel to screen potential participants or to provide certain data). In many cases, the evaluator does not have the clout necessary to obtain the needed commitments. The funding agency may be in a better position to approach local agencies (e.g., police, corrections, schools) to obtain their cooperation.

Despite the best efforts to ensure a sound and feasible plan for the evaluation, some impact evaluations will encounter major problems. However, some of those evaluations may nonetheless be salvageable if additional resources are available for the efforts required to overcome the problems. For example, in a multisite trial of domestic violence programs, one site may experience major difficulties unrelated to the study and be forced to close or considerably reduce its services. Potential replacement sites might be available, but the investigator may not have funds for recruitment and start-up in a new site. In this situation, augmenting the award with the funds necessary to add the replacement sites may be a more cost-effective option than allowing a diminished study to go forward. To cover such eventualities, agencies must maintain an emergency fund as a component of their budgeting for evaluation projects with well-specified procedures and guidelines for using it. Such a fund will be counterproductive, however, if it is not carefully directed toward solvable problems that obstruct what otherwise is a high probability of a successful evaluation project.

STEPS THAT CAN BE TAKEN AFTER AWARDING THE EVALUATION CONTRACT

The typical grant monitoring process requires periodic reporting by the grantee. For larger projects, more intensive monitoring is often used. This process is greatly facilitated when there is a detailed management plan (as described earlier) against which the agency staff can compare actual progress. When such a plan exists, agency staff can take a proactive approach to project monitoring by having telephone conferences at critical times to track the achievement of important milestones and benchmarks. The scale of criminal justice evaluation research is small enough that even one failed evaluation that could have been salvaged through early detection of problems and corrective actions is an important lost opportunity.

For larger and more complex impact evaluations, technical advisory panels incorporated into the monitoring process may expand the range of expertise for anticipating and resolving implementation problems that arise. Agencies might, for instance, use standing committees of researchers—perhaps the same committees that review proposals—to periodically review the scientific aspects of the work and recommend agency responses. Site visits by a technical advisory panel could, for instance, offer valuable advice about recruitment strategies and data collection. As a last resort, the technical panel may suggest early termination of an evaluation to conserve resources for more promising research. Such visiting panels are a standard tool in NIH multisite clinical trial management. Properly conceived and constructed they can be perceived as helpful rather than threatening.

It is common practice to monitor evaluation projects more carefully in the first year than in later years. Although it is clearly important to watch such projects closely in the critical early stages, it is also important to recognize that serious problems can develop in later stages. It is not unusual for evaluation procedures to be circumvented as those associated with a program become more familiar with them. For example, the program staff may learn over time how to manipulate a randomization procedure by altering the order in which cases are presented for randomization. Also, selective reporting to favor the program and even outright falsification of records may slowly creep in. Vigilance throughout the course of the evaluation project is required to catch such changes.

Other mechanisms that can be used to enhance project success after funding include meetings of evaluators of similar projects and cluster conferences for evaluators. Several agencies may use such meetings to provide a forum in which challenges and potential solutions can be discussed. These interactions may be especially helpful when the programs being evaluated are similar, as in multisite projects with different local evaluators.

An extension of this idea is the inclusion of outside expert researchers who are well respected in meetings with the evaluators. Such experts can comment on the progress of the effort and offer helpful advice. These researchers might be members of a standing review committee such as that described earlier who are already familiar with the work. Or, evaluators can simply be put in contact with veteran researchers who have experienced similar challenges in other projects. Of course, many veteran researchers have social networks on which they depend for such advice.

But less experienced researchers or even experienced researchers who are new to a certain type of research would often benefit from consultation with others. Agencies might maintain a directory of experienced researchers who could be called upon to consult with grantees as situations arise. Advisory boards are often created for this purpose and may be especially helpful on large and complex projects.

6

What Organizational Infrastructure and Procedures Support High-Quality Evaluation?

Adequate funding is a prerequisite for sustaining a critical mass of timely and high-quality impact evaluations distributed over the criminal justice programs of national and regional policy interest. Relative to the resources devoted to studying the effectiveness of interventions in health and education, those available from all sources for evaluation of criminal justice programs are meager (Sherman 2004). This limitation constrains the potential quantity of criminal justice program evaluation and inhibits allocation of sufficient funding for high-quality research in any given evaluation project. The reality of this constraint makes it especially important for any agency funding criminal justice evaluation to prioritize evaluation projects in ways that provide the greatest amount of credible and useful information for each investment.

Effective prioritizing, in turn, requires a funding agency to maintain a strategic planning function designed to focus evaluation resources where they will make the most difference. Such planning must include an ongoing effort to scan the horizon for pertinent policy issues and identify emerging information needs, survey the field, and assess prospects for evaluation. In is not sufficient, however, to only monitor the state of the science and literature in criminal justice. The evolving political agenda must be understood as well so that policy makers' need for information about criminal justice programs can be anticipated to the extent possible.

One important organizational implication of this circumstance is that agencies supporting evaluation research must have effective ongoing mechanisms for obtaining input from practitioners, policy makers, and researchers about priorities for program evaluation. Typical procedures for accomplishing this include scanning of relevant information sources and interaction with networks of key informants by knowledgeable program staff, consultation via advisory boards or study groups, and strategic planning studies.

As mentioned in the previous chapter, it may be problematic to combine the functions of setting priorities for program evaluation with those of reviewing proposals for evaluation of specific programs. Practitioner and policy maker perspectives are critical to setting priorities that advance practice and policy, but of limited value for assessing the quality of proposed evaluation research. Conversely, the current state of research evidence about criminal justice programs, especially emerging and innovative ideas, is relevant to strategic planning for evaluation but the perspective of researchers on what best serves practice and policy is generally limited.

Obtaining well-informed and thoughtful input from practitioners, policy makers, and researchers in their respective areas of expertise requires that an agency have ready access to quality consultants and reviewers. Moreover, those consultants and reviewers must be willing to serve on advisory boards, review panels, and the like. It follows that an agency that wishes to set effective priorities and sponsor high-quality program evaluation must include personnel who maintain networks of contacts with outside experts and attend to the incentives that encourage such persons to participate in the pertinent agency processes. Correspondingly, the relevant staff must be supported with opportunities for participation in conferences and similar events that allow personal interactions and monitoring of developments in the field. They must also have time within the scope of their official duties to monitor and assimilate information from the respective research, practitioner, and policy literatures.

AGENCY STAFF RESPONSIBLE FOR EVALUATION

Given well-developed priorities for evaluation, the functions related to developing and supporting quality evaluations include more than the ability to assemble and work with qualified review panels. As discussed in the previous chapter, formulation of an RFP that provides clear and detailed guidance for development of strong evaluation proposals, and the preliminary site visits, feasibility studies, or evaluability assessments that may be necessary to do that well can also be significant to the ultimate quality and successful implementation of impact evaluations. After an evaluation is commissioned, knowledgeable participation in the monitoring process is also an important function for the responsible agency personnel. In addition, such personnel may be expected to respond to questions from policy makers and practitioners about research evidence for the effectiveness of the programs evaluated. For instance, staff may be asked to provide an assessment of what interventions are thought to work and what promising new interventions are on the horizon.

These various functions are best undertaken by staff members who understand research methodology and the underlying principles of the interventions. Moreover, given the diverse methods applicable to the evaluation of criminal justice programs, it would be an advantage for the responsible staff members to have broad research training and not be strongly identified with any particular methodological camp. The selection of personnel for these positions is an important agency function. Opportunities for appropriate professional development, such as further methodological training or short-term placement in other funding agencies, may also be beneficial to enable staff to stay current with methodological and conceptual advances in the field. Other ways of enhancing the evaluation and program expertise resident in the agency include hosting outside experts as visiting fellows, supporting advanced graduate student interns, and regular engagement with a standing advisory board.

High-quality evaluation research occurs most readily in an organizational context in which the culture and leadership clearly value and nurture such research and the associated concept of evidence-based decision-making (GAO, 2003b; Garner and Visher, 2003; Palmer and Petrosino, 2003). This support includes attracting and retaining well-qualified professional staff, encouraging the sharing and use of information, and proactively identifying opportunities to push the evidence base in the direction of decision-making priorities. These considerations, and those discussed above, suggest that sound evaluation will be best developed and administered through a designated evaluation unit with clear responsibility for the quality of the resulting projects. To function effectively in this role, such a unit needs a dedicated budget and relative independence from program and political influence that might compromise the integrity of the evaluation research. Such a unit would also require staff with research backgrounds as well as practical experience and sufficient continuity to develop expertise in the essential functions particular to the programs and evaluations of the agency.

RELATIONSHIPS WITH OTHER AGENCIES AND EVALUATION OPPORTUNITIES

Given limited resources for evaluating criminal justice programs and policies, opportunities for agencies to leverage resources through collaborative relationships with other organizations offer potential advantages. One direct approach is through partnerships for sponsoring evaluation with organizations that share those interests. Many criminal justice topics, such as substance abuse and violence, are of interest to federal agencies and foundations outside the ambit of the National Institute of Justice, the major federal funder of criminal justice evaluation research. Other organizations, such as the Campbell Collaboration, engage in evaluation activities that routinely involve networks of prominent researchers and relevant organizations.

An especially productive form of collaboration occurs when a high-quality evaluation can "piggy back" on funding for a criminal justice service program. Funding for service programs often includes support for evaluation and data collection, and may even require it. Supplements that enhance the quality and utility of these embedded evaluations in selected circumstances are a cost-effective strategy for maximizing the value of research dollars. These opportunities can be developed by building collaborative relationships with agencies and units that fund service programs and may have the additional advantage of helping promote evaluation as a standard practice rather than a unique event. It should be noted that such interaction between service funding and evaluation implementation is in keeping with the increased advocacy for evidence-based policy that has occurred in recent years.

Impact evaluations frequently involve collaboration with the criminal justice programs being evaluated. However, the programs are often not enthusiastic collaborators and, in many instance, evaluators must seek programs willing to volunteer to participate in the evaluation. Difficulty in recruiting such reluctant volunteers, as noted earlier, is one of the recurring problems of implementation for impact evaluations. In this context, a critical function for an agency sponsoring impact evaluation is finding ways to ensure the participation of the programs for which evaluation is desired. The most effective procedure is for program agreement to participate in an external evaluation to be a condition of program funding, even if that option is not always exercised by the evaluation sponsor. Programs that accept external funding but are not willing to be evaluated or, perhaps even actively resist any such attempt, undermine both the development of knowledge about effective programs and the principle of accountability for programs that receive outside funding.

A relevant function for major funders of criminal justice evaluations, therefore, is to exercise what influence and advocacy they can to encourage agencies that fund programs, including their own, to require participation in evaluation when asked unless there are compelling reasons to the contrary. A related function is to facilitate participation by offering effective incentives to the candidate programs and supporting them in ways that help minimize any disruption or inconvenience associated with participation in an impact evaluation.

EFFECTIVE USE OF EVALUATION RESULTS

To influence policy and practice in constructive ways, the findings of impact evaluations must be disseminated in an accessible manner to policy makers and practitioners. A less obvious function, however, is the integration of the findings into the cumulative body of evaluation research in a way that facilitates program improvement and broader knowledge about program effectiveness. This function has several different aspects. Most fundamentally, agencies that sponsor evaluation research must make the results available, with full technical details, to the research community in a timely manner. They may garner praise but, especially for important programs and policies, are at least equally likely to attract criticism. This response may not be gratifying to the sponsoring agency, but the importance of review and discussion of evaluation studies by a critical scientific community cannot be overestimated for purposes of improving evaluation methods and practice as the field evolves.

Potentially encompassed in critical reviews are re-analyses of the data using different models or assumptions and attempts to reconcile divergent findings across evaluation studies. Scrutiny at this level of detail, and the value of what can be learned from that endeavor, of course, are dependent upon access to the data collected in the evaluation. Making such data freely available at an appropriate time and encouraging re-analysis and critique will, in the long run, improve both the evaluations commissioned by the sponsoring agency and general practice in the field. It has the additional value of providing a second (and sometimes third and fourth) opinion about the credibility and utility of evaluation findings that might significantly influence policy or practice. As such, it can reduce the potential for inappropriate use of misleading results.

The value of close review of impact evaluation studies is not confined to those that are successfully implemented and completed. As discussed in Chapter 1, many evaluations fail for reasons of poor design or inadequate implementation. The sponsoring agency and the evaluation field generally can learn much of value for future practice by investigating the circumstances associated with failed evaluations and the problems that led to that failure. For these reasons, it will be useful for an agency to routinely conduct "post-mortems" on unsuccessful projects so that the reasons for failure can be better understood and integrated into the selection and planning of future evaluation projects. To allow comparison and better identification of distinctive sources of problems, similar reviews could be conducted on successful projects as well.

Another consideration regarding the use of evaluation studies has to do with the limitations of individual studies that were discussed in Chapter 4. Impact evaluations, by their nature, are focused on assessing the effects of a particular program at a particular time on particular participants. Any given evaluation thus has limited inherent generalizability. It is for this reason that evaluation researchers and policy makers are increasingly turning to the systematic synthesis or meta-analysis of multiple impact studies of a type of program for robust and generalizable indications of program effectiveness (Petrosino et al., 2003b; Sherman et al., 1997). Contributing studies to such synthesis activities, and providing support to those activities, therefore, are relevant functions for an agency that sponsors significant amounts of impact evaluation research. Indeed, a promising model for managing evaluation research is to combine ongoing research synthesis and meta-analysis by agency staff or contractors, funding of studies in identified gaps in the knowledge base, and occasional larger scale studies in areas where resolving uncertainty is of high value.

DEVELOPING AND SUPPORTING THE TOOLS FOR EVALUATION

Conducting high-quality impact evaluations of criminal justice programs is often hampered by methodological limitations. No one with experience conducting such evaluations would argue that available methods are as fully developed and useful as they could be and even those—such as randomized experiments—that are generally well developed are often difficult to adapt without compromise when applied to operational programs in the field. Moreover, improvements and useful new techniques in evaluation methods in criminal justice are inhibited by limited support for methodological development. A relevant function for any major agency that sponsors impact evaluation, therefore, is to contribute to the improvement of evaluation methods.

There are at least two readily identifiable domains of methodological problems in criminal justice evaluation. One has to do with the availability and adequacy of data for relevant indicators of program outcomes. For criminal justice programs, the outcomes of interest generally have to do with the prevalence of criminal or delinquent offenses or, conversely, victimization. For local data collections, there is little standardization for how such outcomes should be measured and little empirical work to examine how different approaches affect the results. Thus different studies measure recidivism in different ways and over different time periods and varying self-report instruments are used to assess victimization. For evaluation projects that rely on pre-existing data, e.g., crime data from the Uniform Crime Reports (UCR), it is often difficult to find variables that match the specific outcomes of interest and to disaggregate the data to the relevant program site. Multisite studies, in turn, require a common core of data to permit comparison of results across sites, but these must usually be developed ad hoc because there are few standards and little basis for identifying the most relevant measures.

There is much that the agencies that sponsor criminal justice evaluations might do to help alleviate these problems. Most directly, work should be supported on outcome measurement aimed at improving program evaluation and establishing cross-project comparability when possible. It would be especially valuable for evaluation projects if a compendium of scales and items for measuring criminal justice outcomes and the intermediate variables frequently used in criminal justice evaluations could be developed or identified and promoted for general use. Grantees could be asked to select measures from this compendium when appropriate to the evaluation issues. Also, public-use dataset delivery could be incorporated into grant and contract requirements and existing datasets could be expanded to include replication at other sites. Small-scale data augmentation and measurement development projects could be added to large evaluation projects.

The other area in which significant methodological development is needed relates to the research design component of impact evaluations. For the crucial issue of estimating program effects, randomized designs can be difficult to use in many applications and impossible in some and observational studies depend heavily on statistical modeling and assumptions about the influence of uncontrolled variables. Improvements are possible on both fronts. Creative adaptations of randomized designs to operational programs and fuller development of strong quasi-experimental designs, such as regression discontinuity, hold the potential to greatly improve the quality of impact evaluations. Similarly, improvements in statistical modeling and the related area of selection modeling for nonrandomized quasi-experiments could significantly advance evaluation practice in criminal justice.

As with measurement issues, there is much that agencies interested in high-quality impact evaluations could do to advance methodological improvement in evaluation design, and at relatively modest cost. Design-side studies could be added to large evaluation projects; for instance, small quasi-experimental control groups of different sorts to compare with randomized controls and supplementary data collections that allowed exploration of potentially important control variables for statistical modeling. Where small-scale or pilot evaluation studies are appropriate, innovative designs could be tried out to build more experience and better understanding of them. Secondary analysis of existing data and simulations with contrived data could also be supported to explore certain critical design issues. In similar spirit, meta-analysis of existing studies could be undertaken with a focus on methodological influences in contrast to the typical meta-analytic orientation to program effects.

7

Summary, Conclusions, and Recommendations: Priorities and Focus

Effective policy in many areas of criminal justice depends on the ability of various programs to reduce crime or protect potential victims. However, evaluations of criminal justice programs will not have practical and policy significance if the programs are not sufficiently well-developed for the results to have generality or no audience is interested in the results. Moreover, questions about program effects, which are usually those with the greatest generality and potential practical significance, are not necessarily appropriate for all programs. Allocating limited evaluation resources productively, therefore, requires careful prioritizing of the programs to be evaluated and the questions to be asked about their performance. This observation leads to the following recommendations:

- Agencies that sponsor and fund evaluations of criminal justice programs should routinely assess and prioritize the evaluation opportunities within their scope. Resources should mainly be directed toward programs for which there is (a) the greatest potential for practical and policy significance from the knowledge expected to result and (b) the circumstances are amenable to research capable of producing the intended knowledge. Priorities for evaluation should also include consideration of the evaluation questions most important to answer (e.g., process or impact) and the aspect(s) of the program on which to focus the evaluation.
- For public agencies such as the National Institute of Justice, that process should involve input from practitioners and policy makers, as well as researchers, about the practical significance of the knowledge likely to be generated from evaluations of various types of criminal jus-

tice programs and the appropriate priorities to apply. However, this is distinct from assessment of specific proposals for evaluation that respond to those priorities, a task for which the expertise of practitioners and policy makers is poorly suited relative to that of experienced evaluation researchers.

BACKGROUND CHECK FOR PROGRAMS CONSIDERED FOR EVALUATION

There are many preconditions for an impact evaluation of a criminal justice program to have a reasonable chance of producing valid and useful knowledge. The program must be sufficiently well-defined to be replicable, the program circumstances and personnel must be amenable to an evaluation study, the requirements of the research design must be attainable (appropriate samples, data, comparison groups, and the like), the political environment must be stable enough for the program to be maintained during the evaluation, and a research team with adequate expertise must be available to conduct the evaluation. These preconditions cannot be safely assumed to hold for any particular program nor can an evaluation team be expected to locate and recruit a program that meets these preconditions if it has not been identified in advance of commissioning the evaluation. Moreover, once the program to be evaluated has been identified, certain key information about its nature and circumstances is necessary to develop an evaluation design that is feasible to implement.

It follows that a sponsoring agency cannot launch an impact evaluation with reasonable prospects for success unless the specific program to be evaluated has been identified and background information gathered about the feasibility of evaluation and what considerations must be incorporated into the design. Recommendations:

• The requisite background work may be done by an evaluator proposing an evaluation prior to submitting the proposal. Indeed, evaluators occasionally find themselves in fortuitous circumstances where conditions are especially favorable for a high-quality impact evaluation. To stimulate and capitalize on such situations, sponsoring agencies should devote some portion of the funding available for evaluation to support (a) researchers proposing early stages of evaluation that address issues of priority, feasibility, and evaluability and (b) opportunistic funding of impact evaluations proposed by researchers who find themselves in circumstances where a strong evaluation of a significant criminal justice program can be conducted.

• The requisite background work may be instigated by the agency sponsoring the evaluation of selected programs. To accomplish this, agencies should support feasibility or design studies that assess the prospects for a successful impact evaluation of each program of interest. Appropriate preliminary investigations might include site visits, pipeline studies, piloting data collection instruments and procedures, evaluability assessments and the like. The results of these studies should then be used to identify program situations where funding a full impact study is feasible and warranted.

• The preconditions for successful impact evaluation can generally be most easily attained when they are built into a program from the start. Agencies that sponsor program initiatives should consider which new programs may be significant candidates for impact evaluation. The program initiative should then be configured to require or encourage as much as possible the inclusion of the well-defined program structures, record keeping and data collection, documentation of program activities, and other such components supportive of an eventual impact evaluation.

SOUND EVALUATION DESIGN

Within the range of recognized research designs capable of assessing program effects, there are inherent trade-offs that keep any one from being optimal for all circumstances. Careful consideration of the match between the design and the program circumstances and evaluation purposes is required. Moreover, that consideration must be well-informed and thoughtfully developed before an evaluation plan is accepted and implemented. Although there are no simple answers to the question of which designs best fit which evaluation problems, some guidelines can be applied when considering the approach to be used for a particular impact evaluation.

• When requesting an impact evaluation, the sponsoring agency should specify as completely as possible the evaluation questions to be answered, the program sites expected to participate, the outcomes of interest, and the preferred methods to be used. These specifications should be informed by background information of the type described above.

• Development of the specifications for an impact evaluation (e.g., an RFP) and the review of proposals for conducting it should involve expert panels of evaluation researchers with diverse methodological backgrounds and sufficient opportunity for them to explore and discuss the trade-offs and potential associated with different approaches. The members of these panels should be selected to represent evaluators whose own work represents high methodological standards to avoid perpetuating the weaker strands of evaluation practice in criminal justice.

• Given the state of criminal justice knowledge, randomized experimental designs should be favored in situations where it is likely that they can be implemented with integrity and will yield useful results. This is particularly the case where the intervention is applied to units for which assignment to different conditions is feasible, e.g., individual persons or clusters of moderate scope such as schools or centers.

• Before an impact evaluation design is implemented, the assumptions upon which its validity depends should be made explicit, the data and analyses required to support credible conclusions about program effects should be identified, and the availability of the required data should be demonstrated. This is especially important when observational or quasi-experimental studies are used. Meeting the assumptions that are required to produce results with high internal validity in such studies is difficult and requires statistical models that are poorly understood by laypeople and, indeed, many evaluation researchers.

• Research designs for assessing program effects should also address such related matters as the generalizability of those effects, the causal mechanisms that produce them, and the variables that moderate them when feasible.

SUCCESSFUL IMPLEMENTATION OF THE EVALUATION PLAN

Even the most carefully developed designs and plans for impact evaluation may encounter problems when they are implemented that undermine their integrity and the value of their results. Arguably, implementation is a greater barrier to high-quality impact evaluation than difficulties associated with formulating a sound design. High-quality evaluation is most likely to occur when the design is tailored to the respective program circumstances in a way that facilitates adequate implementation, the program being evaluated understands, agrees to, and fulfills its role in the evaluation, and problems that arise during implementation are anticipated and dealt with promptly and effectively. Recommendations:

• A well-developed and clearly-stated RFP is the first step in guarding against implementation failure. An RFP that is based on solid information about the nature and circumstances of the program to be evaluated should encourage prospective evaluators to plan for the likely implementation problems. If the necessary background information to produce a strong RFP is not readily available, agencies should devote sufficient resources during the RFP-development stage to generate it. Site visits, evaluability assessments, pilot studies, pipeline analyses, and other such preliminary investigations are recommended.

- The application review process can also be used to enhance the quality of implementation of funded evaluations. Knowledgeable reviewers can contribute not only to the selection of sound evaluation proposals but to improving the methodological quality and potential for successful implementation of those selected. In order to strengthen the quality of application reviews, a two-stage review is recommended whereby the policy relevance of the programs under consideration for evaluation are first judged by knowledgeable policy makers, practitioners, and researchers. Proposals that pass this screen then receive a scientific review from a panel of well-qualified researchers. The review panels at this second stage focus solely on the scientific merit and likelihood of successful implementation of the proposed research.

- The likelihood of a successful evaluation is greatly diminished when it is imposed on programs that have not agreed voluntarily or as a condition of funding to participate. Plans and commitments for impact evaluation should be built into the design of programs during their developmental phase whenever possible. When the agency sponsoring the evaluation also provides funding for the program being evaluated, the terms associated with that funding should include participation in an evaluation if selected and specification of recordkeeping and other program procedures necessary to support the evaluation. Commissioning an evaluation for which the evaluator must then find and recruit programs willing to participate should be avoided. This practice not only compromises the generalizability of the evaluation results, but it makes the success of the evaluation overly dependent upon the happenstance circumstances of the volunteer programs and their willingness to continue their cooperation as the evaluation unfolds.

- A detailed management plan should be developed for implementation of an impact evaluation that specifies the key events and activities and associated timeline for both the evaluation team and the program. To ensure that the role of the program and other critical partners is understood and documented, memoranda of understanding should be drafted and formally agreed to by the major parties.

- Knowledgeable staff of the sponsoring agency should monitor the implementation of the evaluation, e.g., through conference calls and periodic meetings with the evaluation team. Where appropriate the agency may need to exercise its influence directly with local program partners to ensure that commitments to the evaluation are honored.

- Especially for larger projects, implementation and problem solving may be facilitated by support to the evaluation team in such forms as meetings or cluster conferences of evaluators with similar projects for the purpose of cross-project sharing and learning or consultation with advisory groups of veteran researchers.

• When arranging funding for impact evaluation projects, the sponsoring agency should set aside an emergency fund to be used on an as-needed basis to respond to unexpected problems and maintain implementation of an otherwise promising evaluation project.

IMPROVING THE TOOLS FOR EVALUATION RESEARCH

The research methods for conducting impact evaluation, the data resources needed to adequately support it, and the integration and synthesis of results for policy makers and researchers are all areas where the basic tools need further development to advance high-quality evaluation of criminal justice programs. Agencies such as NIJ with a major investment in evaluation should devote a portion of available funds to methodological development in areas such as the following:

• Research aimed at adapting and improving impact evaluation designs for criminal justice applications; for example, development and validation of effective applications of alternative designs such as regression-discontinuity, selection bias models for nonrandomized comparisons, and techniques for modeling program effects with observational data.
• Development and improvement of new and existing databases in ways that would better support impact evaluation of criminal justice programs and measurement studies that expand the repertoire of relevant outcome variables and knowledge about their characteristics and relationships for purposes of impact evaluation (e.g., self-report delinquency and criminality, official records of arrests, convictions, and the like, measures of critical mediators).
• Synthesis and integration of the findings of impact evaluations in ways that inform practitioners and policy makers about the effectiveness of different types of criminal justice programs and the characteristics of the most effective programs of each type and that inform researchers about gaps in the research and the influence of methodological variation on evaluation results.

ORGANIZATIONAL SUPPORT FOR
HIGH-QUALITY EVALUATION

To support high-quality impact evaluation, the sponsoring agency must itself incorporate sufficient expertise to help set effective and feasible evaluation priorities, accomplish the background preparation necessary to develop the specifications for evaluation projects, monitor implementation, and work well with expert advisory boards and review panels. Maintaining such resident expertise, in turn, requires an organizational commitment to evaluation research and evidence-based decision making within a culture of respect for these functions and the personnel responsible for carrying them out. Recommendations:

- Agencies such as NIJ that sponsor a significant portfolio of evaluation research in criminal justice should maintain a separate evaluation unit with clear responsibility for developing and completing high-quality evaluation projects. To be effective, such a unit will need a dedicated budget, a certain amount of authority over the evaluation research budgets and project selection, and independence from undue program and political influence on the nature and implementation of the evaluation projects undertaken.

- The agency personnel responsible for developing and overseeing impact evaluation projects should include individuals with relevant research backgrounds who are assigned to evaluation functions and maintained in those positions in ways that ensure continuity of experience with the challenges of criminal justice evaluation, methodological developments, and the community of researchers available to conduct quality evaluations.

- The unit and personnel responsible for developing and completing evaluation projects should be supported by review and advisory panels that provide expert consultation in developing RFPs, reviewing evaluation proposals and plans, monitoring the implementation of evaluation studies, and other such functions that must be performed well in order to facilitate high-quality evaluation research.

References

Ayres, I., and S. Levitt, S.
  1998 Measuring positive externalities from unobservable victim precaution: An empirical analysis of LOJACK. *Quarterly Journal of Economics* 113(1):43-77.
Berk, R.
  1992 The differential deterrent effects of an arrest in incidents of domestic violence: A Bayesian analysis of four randomized field experiments (with Alec Campbell, Ruth Klap and Bruce Western). *American Sociological Review* 5(57):689-708.
  2003 Conducting a Randomized Field Experiment for the California Department of Corrections: The Experience of the Inmate Classification Experiment. Paper presented at the Workshop on Improving Evaluation of Criminal Justice Programs, September 5, National Research Council, Washington DC. Available: http://www7.nationalacademies.org/CLAJ/Evaluation%20-%20Richard%20Berk.pdf.
Braga, A.
  2003 Hot Spots Policing and Crime Prevention: Evidence from Five Randomized Controlled Trials. Paper presented at the Workshop on Improving Evaluation of Criminal Justice Programs, September 5, National Research Council, Washington DC. Available: http://www7.nationalacademies.org/CLAJ/Evaluation%20-%20 Anthony% 20Braga.doc.
Brainard, J.
  2001 The wrong rules for social science? *The Chronicle of Higher Education*, March 9, A21.
Brown, S.
  1989 Statistical power and criminal justice research. *Journal of Criminal Justice* 17: 115-122.
Chamberlain, P.
  2003 The Benefits and Hazards of Conducting Community-Based Randomized Trials: Multidimensional Treatment Foster Care as a Case Example. Paper presented at the Workshop on Improving Evaluation of Criminal Justice Programs, September 5, National Research Council, Washington DC. Available: http://www7.nationalacademies.org/CLAJ/Evaluation%20-%20Patricia%20Chamberlain.doc.

Cohen, J.
   1988   *Statistical Power Analysis for the Behavioral Sciences* (2nd ed.). Hillsdale, NJ: Lawrence Erlbaum Associates.
Cook, T., and D. Campbell
   1979   *Quasi-Experimentation: Design and Analysis Issues for Field Settings*. Boston, MA: Houghton Mifflin Company.
Cook, P.J., and G. Tauchen
   1984   The effect of minimum drinking age legislation on youthful auto fatalities, 1970-1977. *Journal of Legal Studies* 13:169-190.
Cooper, H.M.
   1998   *Synthesizing Research: A Guide for Literature Reviews* (3rd ed.). (Applied Social Research Methods Series 2.) Thousand Oaks, CA: Sage.
Cooper, H.M., and LV. Hedges
   1994   *The Handbook of Research Synthesis*. New York: Russell Sage Foundation.
Eck, J.
   2002   Learning from experience in problem oriented policing and crime prevention: The positive function of weak evaluations and the negative functions of strong ones. Pp. 93-117 in N. Tilley (ed.), *Evaluation for Crime Prevention: Crime Prevention Studies* (vol. 14). Monsey, NY: Criminal Justice Press.
Farrington, D.P., and B.C. Welsh
   2002   Improved street lighting and crime prevention. *Justice Quarterly* 19(2):313-331.
Feder, L., and R. Boruch
   2000   The need for randomized experimental designs in criminal justice settings. *Crime and Delinquency* 46(3):291-294.
Fleiss, J.
   1982   Multicenter clinical trials: Bradford Hill's contributions and some subsequent developments. *Statistics in Medicine* 1:353-359.
Garner, J., J. Fagan, and C. Maxwell
   1995   Published findings from the spouse assault replication program: A critical review. *Journal of Quantitative Criminology* 11(1):3-28.
Garner, J.H., and C.A. Visher
   2003   The production of criminological experiments. *Evaluation Review* 27(3):316-335.
Glasgow, R.E., T.M. Vogt, and S.M. Boles
   1999   Evaluating the public health impact of health promotion interventions: The RE-AIM framework. *American Journal of Public Health* 89:1323-1327.
Gottfredson, D.C., K. Kumpfer, D. Polizzi-Fox, D. Wilson, V. Puryear, P. Beatty, and M. Vilmenay
   2004   Challenges in disseminating model programs: A qualitative analysis of the Strengthening Washington DC Families Project. *Clinical Child and Family Psychology Review* 7(3):165-176.
Heckman, J., and R. Robb
   1985   Alternative methods for evaluating the impact of interventions. In J. Heckman and B. Singer (eds.), *Longitudinal Analysis of Labor Market Data*. Cambridge, England: Cambridge University Press.
Herrell, J.M., and R.B. Straw
   2002   *Conducting Multiple Site Evaluations in Real-World Settings*. (New Directions for Evaluation No. 94.) San Francisco, CA: Jossey-Bass.
Kelling, G.L., T. Pate, D. Dieckman, and C.E. Brown
   1974   *The Kansas City Preventive Patrol Experiment: Technical Report*. Washington, DC: Police Foundation.

Kunz, R., and A. Oxman
    1998   The unpredictability paradox: Review of the empirical comparisons of random-ized and nonrandomized clinical trials. *British Medical Journal* 317:1185-1190.
Lipsey, M.
    2000   Statistical conclusion validity for intervention research: A significant (p <.05) prob-lem. In L. Bickman (ed.), *Validity and Social Experimentation: Donald Campbell's Legacy*. Thousands Oaks, CA: Sage.
Lipsey, M., and D. Wilson
    2001   *Practical Meta-Analysis*. (Applied Social Research Methods Series Vol. 49.) Thou-sand Oaks, CA: Sage.
Logan, C.H., and G.G. Gaes
    1993   Meta-analysis and the rehabilitation of punishment. *Justice Quarterly* 10:245-263.
Ludwig, J., and P.J. Cook
    2000   Homicide and suicide rates associated with implementation of the Brady Hand-gun Violence Prevention Act. *Journal of the American Medical Association* 284:585-591.
MacKenzie, D., and C. Souryal
    1994   *Multisite evaluation of shock incarceration: Evaluation report*. Washington, DC: Na-tional Institute of Justice.
Manski, C.
    1995   *Identification Problems in the Social Sciences*. Cambridge, MA: Harvard University Press.
    1996   Learning about treatment effects from experiments with random assignment of treatment. *Journal of Human Resources* 31(4):707-733.
Manski, C., and D. Nagin
    1998   Bounding disagreements about treatment effects: A case study of sentencing and recidivism. *Sociological Methodology* 28:99-137.
National Research Council
    2001   *Informing America's Policy on Illegal Drugs: What We Don't Know Keeps Hurting Us*. Committee on Data and Research for Policy on Illegal Drugs. C.F. Manski, J.V. Pepper, and C.V. Petrie, eds. Committee on Law and Justice and Committee on National Statistics. Commission on Behavioral and Social Sciences and Education. Washington, DC: National Academy Press.
    2004   *Fairness and Effectiveness in Policing: The Evidence*. Committee to Review Research on Police Policy and Practices. W. Skogan and K. Frydl, eds. Committee on Law and Justice, Division of Behavioral and Social Sciences and Education. Washing-ton, DC: The National Academies Press.
    2005   *Firearms and Violence: A Critical Review*. Committee to Improve Research Informa-tion and Data on Firearms. C.F. Wellford, J.V. Pepper, and C.V. Petrie, eds. Com-mittee on Law and Justice, Division of Behavioral and Social Sciences and Educa-tion. Washington, DC: The National Academies Press.
National Research Council and Institute of Medicine
    2001   *Juvenile Crime, Juvenile Justice*. Panel on Juvenile Crime: Prevention, Treatment, and Control. J. McCord, C. Spatz Widom, and N.A. Crowell, eds. Committee on Law and Justice and Board on Children, Youth, and Families. Washington, DC: National Academy Press.
Oakes, J.M.
    2002   Risks and wrongs in social science research. *Evaluation Review* 26(5):443-479.
Palmer, T., and A. Petrosino
    2003   The experimenting agency: The California Youth Authority Research Division. *Evaluation Review* 27(3):228-266.

Pawson, R., and N. Tilley
  1997   *Realistic Evaluation.* Thousand Oaks, CA: Sage.
Petersilia, J., and S. Turner
  1993   Intensive probation and parole. Pp. 281-335 in M. Tonry (ed.), *Crime and Justice: A Review of Research* (vol. 19). Chicago, IL: The University of Chicago Press.
Petrosino, A., C. Turpin-Petrosino, and J. Buehler
  2003a   Scared Straight and other juvenile awareness programs for preventing juvenile delinquency: A systematic review of the randomized experimental evidence. *Annals of the American Academy of Political and Social Science* 589:41-62.
Petrosino, A., R.F. Boruch, D.P. Farrington, L.W. Sherman, and D. Weisburd
  2003b   Toward evidence-based criminology and criminal justice: Systematic reviews, the Campbell Collaboration, and the Crime and Justice Group. *International Journal of Comparative Criminology* 3(1):42-61.
Rossi, P.H., M.W. Lipsey, and H.E. Freeman
  2004   *Evaluation: A Systematic Approach* (7th ed.). Thousand Oaks, CA: Sage.
Rydell, C.P., and S.S. Everingham
  1994   *Controlling Cocaine: Supply Versus Demand Programs.* Santa Monica, CA: RAND.
Shadish, W., T. Cook, and D. Campbell
  2002   *Experimental and Quasi-experimental Designs for Generalized Causal Inferences.* Boston, MA: Houghton-Mifflin Company.
Sherman, L.D.
  1992   *Policing Domestic Violence: Experiments and Dilemmas.* New York: Free Press.
  2004   Research and policing: The infrastructure and political economy of federal funding. *Annals of the American Academy of Political and Social Science* 593:156-178.
Sherman, L.D., and D. Weisburd
  1995   General deterrent effects of police patrol in crime "hot spots": A randomized study. *Justice Quarterly* 12(4).
Sherman, L., D. Farrington, B. Welsh, and D. MacKenzie (eds.)
  2002   *Evidence-Based Crime Prevention.* London, England: Routledge.
Sherman, L., D. Gottfredson, D. MacKenzie, J. Eck, P. Reuter, and S. Bushway
  1997   *Preventing Crime: What Works, What Doesn't, What's Promising: A Report to the United States Congress.* Washington, DC: National Institute of Justice.
Stanley, K., M. Stjernsward, and M. Isley
  1981   *The Conduct of a Cooperative Clinical Trial.* New York: Springer-Verlag.
Tilley, N.
  1994   *After Kirkhold—Theory, Method and Results of Replication Evaluations.* (Police Research Group, Crime Prevention Unit Series Paper No. 47.) London, England: Home Office Police Department.
Todd, P.
  2003   Alternative Methods of Evaluating Anti-Crime Programs. Paper presented at the Workshop on Improving Evaluation of Criminal Justice Programs, September 5, National Research Council, Washington DC. Available: http://nrc51/xpedio/groups/dbasse/documents/webpage/027646%7E2.doc.
U.S. General Accounting Office
  2001   *Juvenile Justice: OJJDP Reporting Requirements for Discretionary and Formula Grantees and Concerns about Evaluation Studies.* Washington, DC: U.S. Government Printing Office.
  2002a   *Drug Courts: Better DOJ Data Collection and Evaluation Efforts Needed to Measure Impact of Drug Court Programs.* Washington, DC: U.S. Government Printing Office.

2002b   *Justice Impact Evaluations: One Byrne Evaluation Was Rigorous; All Reviewed Violence Against Women Office Evaluations Were Problematic.* Washington, DC: U.S. Government Printing Office.

2002c   *Violence Against Women Office: Problems with Grant Monitoring and Concerns about Evaluation Studies.* Washington, DC: U.S. Government Printing Office.

2003a   *Justice Outcome Evaluations: Design and Implementation of Studies Require More NIJ Attention.* Washington, DC: U.S. Government Printing Office.

2003b   *Program Evaluation: An Evaluation Culture and Collaborative Partnerships Help Build Agency Capacity.* Washington, DC: U.S. Government Printing Office.

Wagenaar, A.
1999   Communities mobilizing for change on alcohol. *Journal of Community Psychology* 27(3):315-326.

Weisburd, D.
2003   Ethical practice and evaluation of interventions in crime and justice: The moral imperative for randomized trials. *Evaluation Review* 27(3):336-354.

Weisburd, D., and F. Taxman
2000   Developing a multicenter randomized trial in criminology: The case of HIDTA. *Journal of Quantitative Criminology* 16(3):315-340.

Weisburd, D., A. Petrosino, and G. Mason
1993   Design sensitivity in criminal justice experiments. In M. Tonry (ed.) *Crime and Justice: A Review of Research* (vol. 17). Chicago, IL: University of Chicago Press.

Weisburd, D., C.M. Lum, and S.M. Yang
2002   When can we conclude that treatments or programs don't work? *The Annals of the American Academy of Political and Social Science* 587:31-48.

Weiss, C.H.
1998   *Evaluation* (2nd ed.). Englewood Cliffs, NJ: Prentice Hall.

Wholey, J.S.
1994   Assessing the feasibility and likely usefulness of evaluation. Pp. 15-39 in J.S. Wholey, H.P. Hatry, and K.E. Newcomer (eds.). *Handbook of Practical Program Evaluation.* San Francisco, CA: Jossey-Bass.

Appendix A

Biographical Sketches of Committee Members and Staff

MARK W. LIPSEY (*Chair*) is the director of the Center for Evaluation Research and Methodology and a senior research associate at the Vanderbilt Institute for Public Policy Studies. His professional interests are in the areas of public policy, program evaluation research, social intervention, field research methodology, and research synthesis (meta-analysis). The foci of his recent research have been risk and intervention for juvenile delinquency and issues of methodological quality in program evaluation research. Professor Lipsey serves on the editorial boards of the *Journal of Experimental Criminology, Psychological Bulletin, Evaluation and Program Planning*, and the *American Journal of Community Psychology*, and on boards or committees of the National Research Council, National Institutes of Health, Institute of Education Sciences, Campbell Collaboration, and Blueprints for Violence Prevention. He has received awards for his work from the Society for Prevention Research, American Evaluation Association, Center for Child Welfare Policy, and the American Parole and Probation Association Society and is coauthor of textbooks on program evaluation (*Evaluation: A Systematic Approach*) and meta-analysis (*Practical Meta-Analysis*). He received a Ph.D. in psychology from the Johns Hopkins University in 1972 following a B.S. in applied psychology from the Georgia Institute of Technology in 1968.

JOHN L. ADAMS is a senior statistician in the Statistics Group at the RAND Corporation. His research interests include health care, especially quality measurement systems using both process and outcomes; profiling of health plans, provider groups, and physicians; assessing the quality of care; and the construction and evaluation of simulation models with a special focus on characterization and quantification of sources of uncertainty. He is the author of numerous articles on these topics and, with others, of the book *Public Policy and Statistics: Case Studies* from RAND. For the National Academies Committee on National Statistics, he has served as a committee member for the Panel Study of Data and Methods for Measuring the Effects of Changes in Social Welfare Programs and the Panel to Review Research and Development Statistics at the National Science Foundation.

DENISE C. GOTTFREDSON is a professor at the University of Maryland Department of Criminal Justice and Criminology. Gottfredson's research interests include delinquency and delinquency prevention, and particularly the effects of school environments on youth behavior. Much of Gottfredson's career has been devoted to developing effective collaborations between researchers and practitioners. She directs a project that provides research expertise to the Maryland Governor's Office of Crime Control and Prevention in its efforts to promote effective prevention practices in Maryland. She has recently completed randomized experiments to test the effectiveness of the Baltimore City Drug Treatment Court and the Strengthening Families Program in Washington DC. She is currently directing a randomized trial of the effects of after school programs on the development of problem behavior. She received a Ph.D. in Social Relations from the Johns Hopkins University, where she specialized in Sociology of Education.

JOHN V. PEPPER is associate professor of economics at the University of Virginia. His current work reflects his wide range of interests in social program evaluation, applied econometrics, and public economics. His current work examines such subjects as disability status, teenage childbearing, welfare system rules, and drugs and crime. He is an author of numerous published papers, conference presentations and edited books including several National Research Council reports—*Measurement Problems in Criminal Justice Research* (2003, with Carol Petrie), *Informing America's Policy on Illegal Drugs: What We Don't Know Keeps Hurting Us* (2001, with Charles Manski and Carol Petrie), *Assessment of Two Cost-Effectiveness Studies on Cocaine Control Policy* (1999, with Charles Manski and Yonette Thomas), and *Firearms and Violence: A Critical Review* (2005, with Charles Wellford and Carol Petrie). Professor Pepper received his Ph.D. in economics from the University of Wisconsin-Madison.

DAVID WEISBURD is the Walter E. Mayer Professor of Law and Criminal Justice at Hebrew University Law School in Jerusalem and professor of criminology and criminal justice at the University of Maryland, College Park. He is also a senior fellow at the Police Foundation and chair of its Research Advisory Committee. He has also served as research associate at Yale Law School, senior research associate at the Vera Institute of Justice, associate professor at the School of Criminal Justice at Rutgers University, and director of the Center for Crime Prevention Studies. Professor Weisburd is a fellow of the American Society of Criminology and the Academy of Experimental Criminology. He has served as a principal investigator for a number of federally supported research studies and as a scientific and statistical advisor to local, national, and international organizations. He is author or editor of 11 books and more than 60 scientific articles covering a broad array of topics in crime and justice, including many that deal with methodological or statistical applications in criminal justice research. Professor Weisburd is the founding editor of the *Journal of Experimental Criminology* and coeditor of the *Israel Law Review*. He received his Ph.D. from Yale University.

CAROL V. PETRIE (*Project Director*) is the staff director of the Committee on Law and Justice at the National Research Council, a position she has held since 1997. Prior to that, she was the director of planning and management at the National Institute of Justice, responsible for policy development and administration. In 1994, she served as the acting director of the National Institute of Justice during the transition between the Bush and Clinton administrations. Throughout a 30-year career, she has worked in the area of criminal justice research, statistics, and public policy, serving as a project officer and in administration at the National Institute of Justice and at the Bureau of Justice Statistics. She has conducted research on violence and managed numerous research projects on the development of criminal behavior, policy on illegal drugs, domestic violence, child abuse and neglect, transnational crime, and improving the operations of the criminal justice system. She has a B.S. in education from Kent State University.

Appendix B

Participant List
Workshop on Improving Evaluation of Criminal Justice Programs

Charles Wellford
Department of Criminology and
  Criminal Justice
University of Maryland at College
  Park

John L. Adams
Steering Committee Member
RAND Corporation
Santa Monica, CA

Jay Albanese
National Institute of Justice
Washington, DC

Karen Amendola
Police Foundation
Washington, DC

Bruce Baicar
National Institute of Justice
Washington, DC

Duren Banks
Caliber Associates
Fairfax, VA

Jon Baron
Coalition for Evidence-Based
  Policy
The Council for Excellence in
  Government
Washington, DC

David H. Bayley
School of Criminal Justice
University at Albany, SUNY

Richard Berk
Department of Statistics
University of California, Los
  Angeles

Alfred Blumstein
H. John Heinz III School of Public
  Policy and Management
Carnegie Mellon University
Pittsburgh, PA

Richard Bonnie
Institute of Law, Psychiatry, and
  Public Policy
University of Virginia Law School,
  Charlottesville

Anthony Braga
Kennedy School of Government
Harvard University
Cambridge, MA

Henry Brownstein
National Institute of Justice
Washington, DC

Scott Camp
Federal Bureau of Prisons
Washington, DC

Patricia Chamberlain
Oregon Social Learning Center,
  Eugene

Betty Chemers
National Institute of Justice
Washington, DC

Patrick Clark
National Institute of Justice
Washington, DC

Heather Clawson
Caliber Associates
Fairfax, VA

David Clopten
National Institute of Justice
Washington, DC

Martha Crenshaw
Department of Political Science
Wesleyan University
Middleton, CT

Katherine Darke
National Institute of Justice
Washington, DC

Steven Durlauf
Department of Economics
University of Wisconsin–Madison

Laurie Ekstrand
General Accounting Office
Washington, DC

Jeffrey Fagan
School of Law and School of
  Public Health
Columbia University, New York

John Ferejohn
Hoover Institution
Stanford University
Stanford, CA

Thomas Feucht
National Institute of Justice
Washington, DC

Gerald Gaes
National Institute of Justice
Washington, DC

Lisa Gale
National Institute of Justice
Washington, DC

Denise C. Gottfredson
Steering Committee Member
Department of Criminology and
  Criminal Justice
University of Maryland at College
  Park

Adele Harrell
Urban Institute
Washington, DC

Sarah V. Hart
National Institute of Justice
Washington, DC

Doug Horner
National Institute of Justice
Washington, DC

Chris Innes
National Institute of Justice
Washington, DC

Robert L. Johnson
Department of Pediatrics and
    Clinical Psychiatry and
    Department of Adolescent
    and Young Adult Medicine
New Jersey Medical School,
    Newark

Candace Kruttschnitt
Department of Sociology
University of Minnesota,
    Minneapolis

Andrea Lange
National Criminal Justice
    Reference Service
Rockville, MD

John H. Laub
Department of Criminology and
    Criminal Justice
University of Maryland at College
    Park

Mary Layne
Caliber Associates
Fairfax, VA

Steven D. Levitt
Department of Economics
University of Chicago
Chicago, IL

Akiva Liberman
National Institute of Justice
Washington, DC

Mark W. Lipsey
Steering Committee Member
Center for Evaluation Research
    and Methodology
Vanderbilt University
Nashville, TN

Charles Manski
Department of Economics
Northwestern University
Evanston, IL

Catherine McNamee
National Institute of Justice
Washington, DC

Guy Meader
National Institute of Justice
Washington, DC

Lois Mock
National Institute of Justice
Washington, DC

Robert Moffitt
Department of Economics
Johns Hopkins University
Baltimore, MD

Janice Munsterman
National Institute of Justice
Washington, DC

Rosemary Murphy
National Institute of Justice
Washington, DC

Daniel D. Nagin
H. John Heinz III School of Public
    Policy and Management
Carnegie Mellon University
Pittsburgh, PA

Diana Noone
National Institute of Justice
Washington, DC

Angela Moore Parmley
National Institute of Justice
Washington, DC

John V. Pepper
Steering Committee Member
Department of Economics
University of Virginia,
    Charlottesville

Mary Poulin
Juvenile Justice Research Center
Washington, DC

Winnie Reed
National Institute of Justice
Washington, DC

Richard Rosenfeld
Department of Criminology and
    Criminal Justice
University of Missouri-St. Louis

William Sabol
General Accounting Office
Washington, DC

William Saylor
Federal Bureau of Prisons
Washington, DC

Tom Schiller
National Institute of Justice
Washington, DC

Glenn Schmitt
National Institute of Justice
Washington, DC

Lawrence Sherman
Department of Criminology
University of Pennsylvania,
    Philadelphia

Cornelia Sorensen
National Institute of Justice
Washington, DC

Debra Stoe
National Institute of Justice
Washington, DC

Christina Swierczek
National Institute of Justice
Washington, DC

Petra Todd
Department of Economics
University of Pennsylvania,
    Philadelphia

Anita Timrots
National Criminal Justice
    Reference Service
Rockville, MD

Richard Titus
National Institute of Justice
Washington, DC

Al Turner
National Institute of Justice
Washington, DC

Elaine Vaurio
General Accounting Office
Washington, DC

Alex Wagenaar
Alcohol Epidemiology Program
School of Public Health
University of Minnesota,
    Minneapolis

Cheryl Crawford Watson
National Institute of Justice
Washington, DC

David Weisburd
Steering Committee Member
Criminology Department
Hebrew University Law School
Mt. Scopus, Jerusalem, Israel

Ed Zedlewski
National Institute of Justice
Washington, DC

Edward Zigler
Center in Child Development and
    Social Policy
Yale University
New Haven, CT

**National Research Council
Division of Behavioral and Social
Sciences and Education Staff**

Michael J. Feuer
Executive Office

Carol Petrie
Committee on Law and Justice

Jane Ross
Center for Social and Economic
    Studies

Ralph Patterson
Committee on Law and Justice

Brenda McLaughlin
Committee on Law and Justice

Andrew White
Committee on National Statistics

Daniel Cork
Committee on National Statistics